GREAT CARD TRICKS

GREAT CARD TRICKS

BOB LONGE

Sterling Publishing Co., Inc. New York

Library of Congress Cataloging-in-Publication Data

Longe, Bob, 1928–
    Great card tricks / by Bob Longe.
        p.   cm.
    Includes index.
    ISBN 0-8069-3894-3
    1. Card tricks.   I. Title.
GV1549.L528   1995
795.4'38—dc20   95-12702
                                                        CIP

10 9 8 7 6 5 4 3 2 1

Published by Sterling Publishing Company, Inc.
387 Park Avenue South, New York, N.Y. 10016
© 1995 by Bob Longe
Distributed in Canada by Sterling Publishing
% Canadian Manda Group, One Atlantic Avenue, Suite 105
Toronto, Ontario, Canada M6K 3E7
Distributed in Great Britain and Europe by Cassell PLC
Wellington House, 125 Strand, London WC2R 0BB, England
Distributed in Australia by Capricorn Link (Australia) Pty Ltd.
P.O. Box 6651, Baulkham Hills, Business Centre, NSW 2153, Australia
Manufactured in the United States of America
All rights reserved

Sterling ISBN 0-8069-3894-3

CONTENTS

CONTENTS

INTRODUCTION

The purpose of this book is to teach you great card tricks and tell you exactly how to perform them. This includes step-by-step instruction and tips on patter.

You will find here a great variety of card tricks, some of the best of nearly every kind, and you'll get the sleights needed to accomplish almost *any* card trick.

If this book is your introduction to card tricks, it should serve you well. More than one-third of the tricks require no sleight of hand. And several others call for only one easy sleight. Learn several sleights and try out some of the more advanced tricks. With a careful reading and a bit of practice, you may discover that sleight of hand isn't all that difficult, and you'll be ready to astound your friends with a variety of amazing tricks.

If you have some experience with card tricks, you'll find here excellent sleights to add to your repertoire, along with tricks which are varied, unusual, and entertaining.

TIPS

Practice

There are many right ways to perform a card trick. Unfortunately, there are also many wrong ways. You must *know* the trick inside out; the mechanics of it should be almost automatic.

After you've practised on your own, it's time to victimize those close to you—your spouse, your siblings, your intimate friends. You'll discover whether a trick works for you without risking embarrassment before a less friendly audience.

Don't Tell What You're Going to Do

If you announce what you're going to do, you eliminate the element of surprise, but there's even a worse possibility. When you say, "I am going to cause these two cards to change places," spectators are watching for it and stand a better chance of catching you. Occasionally, a trick's effectiveness will depend on your announcing your intention, but this is the exception.

The Effect Is Everything

There's no particular relationship between a trick's difficulty and its effect. Many card artists believe that the more sleights they perform, the better the trick. Actually, the number of sleights is irrelevant. As a performer, you must try to view the trick as the audience does. What does the audience see?

Two cards change places. Does it matter that you used three sleights? If you use one sleight or no sleights, the two cards still change places.

The standard for any trick should be: "Does it deceive, impress, and entertain the audience?"

Tell a Story

Good patter will not only entertain, but will also lead the audience in the wrong direction.

For each trick, then, I recommend that you create some kind of story. You can say that certain cards have an affinity for one another, or that the chosen card is quite obstinate and doesn't like to do what the rest of the cards do, or that this effect has never worked for you before, but that the law of averages should operate in your favor this time.

Don't memorize patter. Instead, have a pretty fair idea of what you want to say and, when you practise, say it in a variety of ways. Memorized patter sounds stilted.

SLEIGHTS

These are the sleights needed to perform certain of the tricks. They can also be used for countless other tricks, perhaps some of your own invention. These sleights are relatively easy, and, when done properly, undetectable. The expert card performer should master a variety of sleights.

Controlling a Card

It's vital that you be able to control a selected card, usually bringing it to the top. Here are five different ways to accomplish this.

Of the following methods of controlling a card, only the *Double-Cut* (below) is a complete cut of the deck. It allows you to bring a card either to the top or the bottom of the deck. The others only control a card to the top. You can easily shuffle the chosen card to the bottom if you wish.

Double-Cut

This is a complete cut of the deck. Suppose you wish to bring a card to the top. Spread the deck for the return of a selected card. The spectator sticks the card into the deck. As you close up the deck, slightly lift the cards above the chosen card with the fingers of your right hand. This will enable you to secure a break with your little finger above the chosen card (Illus. 1). (If the card is to be brought to the bottom, secure a break *below* the selected card.)

Holding the deck from above in your right hand, transfer the break to your right thumb. With your left hand, take some of the cards from the bottom and place them on top (Illus. 2). Take the remainder of the cards below the break

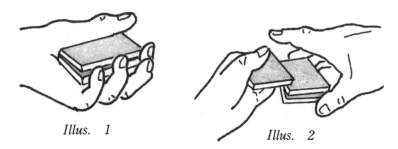

Illus. 1

Illus. 2

and place them on top. (It is perhaps more deceptive if you move three small packets from below the break instead of two.)

This is, by far, the most common way in which magicians control a card to the top or bottom.

As you will see, this is also a sleight which has many other uses in certain tricks.

Delayed Shuffle

You do *not* get a little-finger break when the selected card is returned. Instead, in the process of closing up the deck, you move the cards above the selected card *forward* about half an inch. With your left thumb, push the chosen card to the right. Continuing the process of closing up the deck, move forward the remaining cards in your left hand (Illus. 3). You now have an in-jogged card above the chosen card.

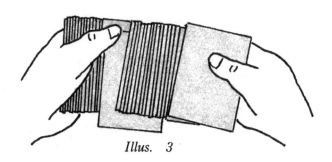

Illus. 3

Immediately drop your left hand with the deck to your side and chat for a moment with the spectators. When you're ready, bring your left hand up in the overhand shuffle position. Your right hand takes the deck, and your right thumb *pushes up* on the protruding card, obtaining a break. Small packets are shuffled into your left hand until the break is reached. All the cards below the break are dropped on top. The chosen card is now on top. (See *Controlling a Group of Cards*, p. 22, for a complete explanation of the overhand shuffle using an in-jogged card. Note particularly Illustrations 11 and 12.)

Simple Overhand Shuffle

Have the spectator place his card on top. False-shuffle the cards and give them a false cut. This works as well as anything else. (See *False Cuts*, p. 17, and *Shuffles*, p. 19.)

Don't Pass It Up

I thought I'd invented this method of bringing a card to the top, but I discovered that Martin Gardner had beaten me to it by a considerable number of years.

A card is selected. As you ask the spectator to show it around, hold the deck in the dealing position in your left hand. Your right hand also holds the cards, gripping them from above with your fingers at the outer end and your thumb at the inner end. With your left fingers, pull the bottom card down about a quarter inch. Your right thumb secures a break between this card and the rest of the deck (Illus. 4). The maneuver is completely covered by your right hand.

Illus. 4

For clarity, the left hand isn't shown.

You're about to perform the first part of a legitimate one-finger cut in preparation for a very tricky move indeed. Bring your left hand behind the deck and, from below with your left forefinger, revolve about half the cards so that they fall into

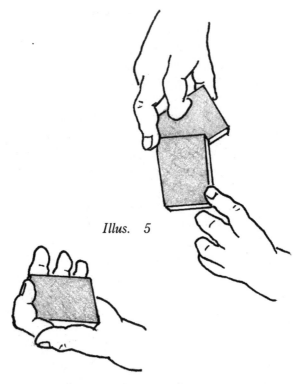

Illus.   5

your hand at the front of the deck (Illus. 5). At this point you're holding half the deck in your left hand, which is in front of your right hand. Extend the cards in your left hand, indicating that the chosen card should be replaced on top. In your right hand is the original lower portion of the deck, at the bottom of which you are holding one card separated with your right thumb.

After the spectator places his card on top of the pile in your left hand, bring the cards in your right hand, ever so briefly, over those in your left hand. Let the bottom card of the packet in your right hand drop on top of the packet in your left hand. As you begin the forward motion of your right hand, say something like, "You had complete freedom of choice, right?" At the beginning of the question, drop the card on top of the packet in your left hand. As you complete the question, continue moving your right hand forward with its packet. Raise your right first finger from the packet and point your finger at the spectator. The whole procedure should appear to be one movement, as you apparently are merely emphasizing your statement by moving the packet forward and pointing a finger at the spectator.

Thumb off the top card of those in your left hand onto the top of those in your right. Place the rest of the cards in your left hand on top of all.

Apparently, you very fairly placed the spectator's card in the middle; actually, it's on top.

Easy Way

Get a little-finger break above the selected card. With your right hand, cut a small pile from the top of the deck. Place the pile face down on the table. Cut off another small pile and place it on top of the pile on the table. Repeat, taking off all the cards above your little-finger break. Finally, place the remaining cards on top of the pile. The chosen card is now on top. It's even more effective if you place the piles on a spectator's outstretched hand.

False Cuts

After a card is returned and brought to the top, it's not a bad idea to further convince spectators that the card is lost by giving the pack a false cut or false shuffle.

False cuts are also very useful when you have a set-up

deck and you want to convince the spectators that the cards are mixed.

Casual Cut

Most versions of this false cut involve a sweeping movement which reveals that *something* peculiar has taken place. Hold the cards in the basic dealing position in your left hand, but with the cards tilted clockwise at about a 45° angle. Approach from the rear with your palm-down right hand. With your right thumb and fingers, grasp approximately the *bottom* half of the deck at the sides. Pull this portion towards you. As soon as the packet clears, lower your left hand a few inches. This creates a compelling illusion that the packet came from the top of the deck. Bring the packet *over* the cards in your left hand and slap it onto the table.

Your right hand, from above, now takes the packet from your left hand. Slap this packet on top of the packet on the table. As you do this, grasp the combined packets and pick them up. Return the complete deck to your left hand.

Multiple-Pile Cut

Set the deck on the table at position "A." Cut off a small portion ("B") and set it somewhat away and to the right of "A." Cut another small pile off "A" and set it to the right of "B"; this is pile "C." Continue with piles "D," "E," "F." Place "B" on "C," place "BC" on "D," and so on to "F." Pick up the combined pile. As an afterthought, notice "A." Place the cards in your hand on "A" and pick all up. The cards are back as they were at the beginning.

Gall Cut

This cut, attributed to Jay Ose, takes a bit of nerve.

With your left thumb riffle down about a third of the deck. Lift off this pile and place it on the table. As you place this pile down, with your left thumb riffle down about half of the remaining cards. Lift these off and place them to the right of the first pile.

Your right hand takes the remaining pile and slaps it down to the right of the other two piles. With your right hand, place the first pile on the second. Pick up the combined pile and place it on the third. The deck is back in its original order.

Shuffles

To perform some of the tricks in this book, you must know how to do two kinds of shuffle, the Hindu shuffle and the overhand shuffle. Neither is difficult, but mastering the *false* overhand shuffle will take some practice.

Hindu Shuffle

With the Hindu shuffle, you can do a variety of sleights. Here, we are just concerned with the mechanics of the shuffle, as well as a very easy force.

Start with the deck in the dealing position in your left hand. With your palm-down right hand, grasp the cards at the near narrow end. Bring the deck towards you with your right hand, allowing your left fingers to draw off a small packet from the top (Illus. 6). This packet falls into your left hand.

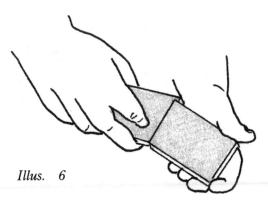

Illus. 6

Draw off another packet, letting it fall onto the one in your left hand. Continue until only a small packet remains in your right hand. Drop this on top of the others.

Now the force: You have your force card on the bottom of the deck. With your first move, you not only withdraw a packet from the top, but you also cling to a small packet on the bottom with your left thumb and left fingers. The packet from the top falls on top of this packet. Complete the shuffle in the usual way. Apparently you've performed a regular Hindu shuffle; actually, the bottom several cards remain exactly as they were. This means, of course, that the force card is still on the bottom. Perform this maneuver a few times.

Ask a spectator to tell you when to stop as you shuffle the cards. Perform the regular Hindu shuffle, taking quite small packets with each move. When the spectator tells you to stop, avert your head and tilt up the packet in your right hand, showing the spectator the bottom card. Then place this packet on top of the cards in your left hand.

Overhand Shuffle
Normal Shuffle

Hold the deck in your left hand as shown in Illus. 7. With your right hand, pick up from the bottom of the deck all but a small packet (Illus. 8). Bring your right hand down (Illus. 9) and let

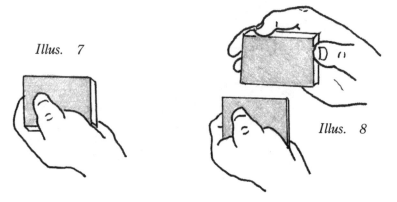

Illus.   7

Illus.   8

a small packet drop from the top of these cards onto the top of the cards in your left hand. Your left thumb lifts a little, allowing passage. The release of these cards from the top of those in your right hand is effected by very slightly relaxing the pressure of your thumb and fingers at the ends.

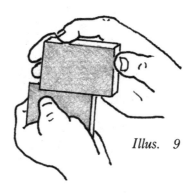

Illus. 9

As the packet is lifted again by your right hand, your left thumb, which was drawn back, returns to the back of the cards being accepted by your left hand. (This is particularly important in the various false shuffles, as you will see.)

Continue dropping packets in the same manner until all the cards are in your left hand.

Bringing the Top Card to the Bottom

In the first move of an overhand shuffle, draw off a single card with your left thumb. Shuffle the rest on top of it. The top card is now on the bottom.

Bringing the Bottom Card to the Top

Start the overhand shuffle. When all that remains in your right hand is a very small packet, draw off cards singly with your left thumb until all have been shuffled off. The bottom card is now on top. (In the same way, you can bring several cards to the top, simply making sure that you draw off the last several cards one at a time.)

Controlling a Group of Cards

The key to all false shuffling is performing casually. Don't stare at your hands. Chat as you do your dirty work.

The idea is to keep a packet on top in order. Again start by picking up from the bottom of the deck all but a small packet. (This small packet will eventually be returned to the top.) As your right hand returns, it's slightly closer to your body. A packet is not released; instead, your left thumb draws off one card. Because your right hand is slightly closer to your body, the card is automatically jogged inward approximately half an inch (Illus. 10). (This move is known as the *injog.*) Your right

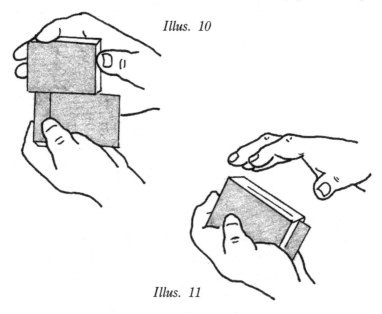

Illus. 10

Illus. 11

hand moves slightly forward; now the cards released into the left hand in small packets will be even with the rest of the deck. At the conclusion of this phase, the deck should look like Illus. 11.

In phase two, as your right hand takes the deck, your thumb pushes up on the protruding card, obtaining a break (Illus. 12). In the overhand shuffle, small packets are dropped into your left hand until the break is reached. All the cards below the break are dropped on top. Thus, the original top packet is back on top.

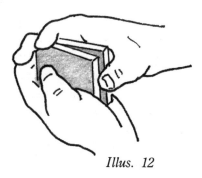

Illus. 12

For clarity, the break is exaggerated.

Forces

Usually, the magician forces a card as an essential part of a trick. Every force, however, can be presented as mind reading. The judicious choice of some of these can enhance a mental routine. When using a force as mind reading, explain that you don't want to influence a spectator psychologically, so the card to be thought of should be chosen completely by chance; then proceed with the force.

Standard Force

The standard force isn't perfect for even the most advanced card expert, but it's well worth learning. No method appears more natural. What's more, if you fail to force a particular card, you simply proceed with a trick where a force isn't required. Any time you do a trick where a card is chosen, try to force a card. The more you practise, the better you'll get. Eventually, you'll be able to force nine times out of ten.

My method is standard, except perhaps for setting up the force card. Clearly, whenever you force a card, you must peek at a card and then get it in position for the force.

To use my method of preparing for the force, you must know how to do the Hindu shuffle (p. 19). Take the deck in the Hindu shuffle position, both hands slightly tilted clockwise. Draw off a small packet in the first move of the Hindu shuffle. As you do so, you are holding most of the deck in your right hand. Turn your right hand even more clockwise until you can see the bottom card (Illus. 13). This is your force card. Now tilt your right hand back to the normal position. Continue drawing off small packets to about half the

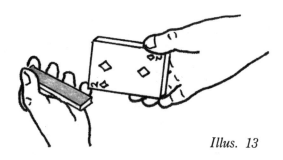

Illus. 13

deck, and then toss the rest of the deck on top, letting the cards fall on top of your inserted little finger, which holds a small break (see Illus. 1, p. 14).

The little finger is now holding a break at the middle of the deck below the card you sighted. Immediately begin to fan the cards into your right hand, pushing with your left thumb on top and pulling with your right fingers underneath. Approach a spectator, saying, "I'd like you to select a card." As he reaches, arrange to have your sighted card fall under his fingertips. How? Coordinate the speed of your fanning and the extension of the deck towards the spectator. Also, you expose the surface of the sighted card a little more as the spectator's hand nears the deck (Illus. 14).

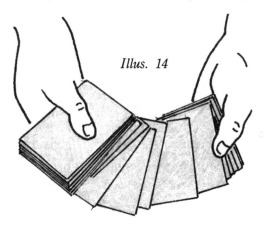

Illus. 14

The surface of the force card is exposed a little more.

If all this seems a bit vague, it is because forcing is more of an art than it is an exact science. There's only one way you'll really get the knack: practising on spectators.

Two Tricks with the Force
Quick Trick
When you successfully force a card, say to the spectator, "Now show the ten of clubs around, but don't let me see it." You'll be quite gratified by the delayed reaction.

Blackstone's Stunt

Harry Blackstone (the elder) used to force a card and, just as the spectator was withdrawing it from the deck, he'd say, "Take any card but the five of spades." When the spectator showed that he indeed had taken the five of spades, Blackstone would express chagrin, and proceed to force it on him again.

Riffle Force

Sneak a peek at the bottom card. Shuffle it to the top in an overhand shuffle. Perform another overhand shuffle, lifting about half the deck with the first move. Draw off one card with your left thumb, injogging the card. Shuffle off the rest. (See *Controlling a Group of Cards*, p. 22.) Place the deck in the dealing position in your left hand. Retaining the deck in your left hand, grip the cards from above with your right hand, fingers at the outer end, thumb at the inner end. As you do so, with the right thumb lift the injogged card. Now you're holding a break above the force card with your right thumb.

Riffle down the left side of the deck a few times with your left thumb. Say to a spectator, "I'd like you to tell me when to stop as I riffle the deck." Slowly riffle down the side of the deck with your left thumb. The spectator will probably tell you to stop somewhere around the middle. If the spectator waits until you're well past the middle, quickly riffle down the remainder of the deck. Start the riffle again, saying, "Tell me to stop anytime." When you're told to stop, tilt the deck slightly forward as you lift off all the cards above the break. Move these cards forward and then to one side. Offer the pile in your left hand, saying, "Take a look at your card, please." Or, if the trick calls for it, say, "Take your card, please, and show it around."

Simon Says

The first person I saw using this force was Simon Lovell; hence, the title.

The top card of the deck is your force card. Hold the deck in the dealing position in your left hand. Fold your left first finger under the deck; this will facilitate the following move. Riffle down the left side of the deck with your left thumb, saying to a spectator, "Tell me when to stop." Stop immediately at the exact point he indicates. Your left thumb now is bending down all the cards below the break (Illus. 15).

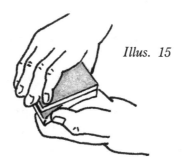

Illus. 15

Hold your right hand palm up next to your left hand. Tilt your left hand clockwise, until the cards above your left thumb fall face up on the extended fingers of your right hand. The right edge of the pile in your right hand should rest along the first joint of your right fingers (Illus. 16). The second

Illus. 16

and third fingers of your left hand flip the pile over so that it falls face down in your right hand. Immediately extend your right hand towards the spectator. Say, "Please look at your card." He looks at the original top card of the deck.

Drop Sleight

This is a wonderful utility move in which one card is secretly exchanged for another. Separate a card at the bottom of the deck, holding a break above it with your right thumb, and then perform the first part of a legitimate one-finger cut: From behind the deck, with your upraised left first finger, revolve about half of the cards from the top of the deck so that they fall into your left hand.

Now for the sleight itself. With your left thumb, push off the top card of those in your left hand. With the left edge of the packet in your right hand, flip this card over so that it turns face up on the lower portion of the deck (Illus. 17). At

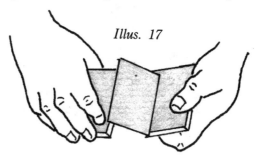

Illus. 17

the conclusion of the move, your right hand, with its packet, swings naturally over the cards in your left hand. Display the card, saying, for instance, "Here we have the six of hearts."

Continue with patter suited to the trick you're doing as you flip the card face down in the same way as you flipped it face up. This time, as your right hand comes over the deck, drop the card separated by your thumb. It falls on top of the lower packet as your right hand continues its sweeping move to the left for an inch or so. This small movement to the left covers the sleight, making it completely invisible.

The original top card of the deck has now been exchanged for the original bottom card of the deck. This maneuver is useful in a number of tricks, as you will see.

Usually, after the sleight is performed, your hands are separated, and the top card of the packet in your left hand is thumbed face down onto the table.

Double-Lift

The double-lift is used in many tricks. A proficient card handler should definitely know how to do one. There are at least a dozen different ways of performing a good double-lift. The three below work extremely well.

Snap Double-Lift

I was told that this was one of John Scarne's favorite methods. I don't know whether he invented it.

Apparently a card is casually snapped face up and flipped back on top of the deck. Actually, it's two cards.

First, you should practise the display of a *single* card by snapping it face up. Incidentally, if you want to make the double-lift believable, always display a card in the same way as you do when performing the sleight.

Hold the deck high in your left hand (Illus. 18). Your right hand lifts off the top card, holding it as shown in Illus. 19. Squeeze the card so that it bevels downwards, as shown in Illus. 20. The idea now is to press down slightly with the first finger and continue bending the card, until by straightening the second finger slightly you snap the card loose from that

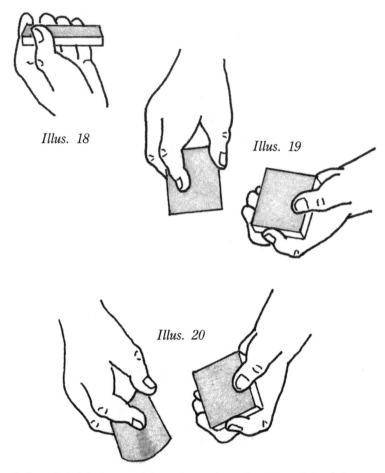

Illus. 18

Illus. 19

Illus. 20

digit and hold the card between your thumb and first finger (Illus. 21). At the same time as you snap the card, turn your hand clockwise so that the card is clearly displayed. The entire move is done in an instant.

The card is returned to the deck by laying its side on the tips of your left hand fingers, and flipping it over with your right hand first finger (Illus. 22).

Practise the entire maneuver until you can do it smoothly and naturally.

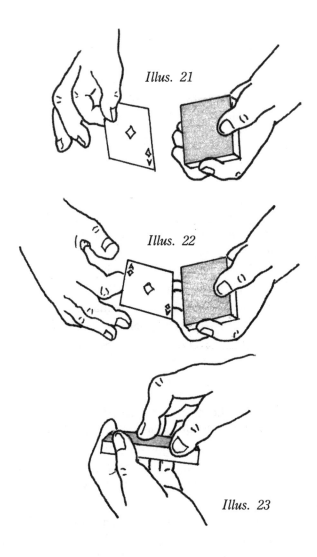

Illus. 21

Illus. 22

Illus. 23

For the double-lift, you duplicate precisely the actions in the single-lift. Holding the deck high in your hand, casually riffle the left side of the deck near the rear with your right thumb (Illus. 23). In doing this, separate the top two cards from the rest of the deck and hold the break with your *left* thumb (Illus. 24).

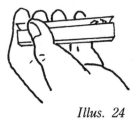

Illus. 24

Take the two cards with your right hand *exactly as you took the single card.* Snap the two cards face up. Name the card. Roll the two back on top. Do all this in precisely the same way as you did the single card.

There's a knack. At first, the cards may separate slightly, but if you treat the two *precisely* as you would a single card, they won't. Alternate snapping over a single card and a double card. Within half an hour, you should have the move mastered.

Efficient Double-Lift

I developed this double-lift some time ago. Since then, I've seen other magicians use double-lifts that are similar, if not identical. I believe that the details make this one of the best: It looks natural, it requires no preparatory move, and the return to the deck is extremely simple.

Hold the deck in your left hand, thumb along the left side. With your right hand, grip the deck from above, thumb at the rear, first finger folded on top, and the remaining fingers at the outer end (Illus. 25).

Bevel the cards back slightly. With your right thumb, lift two cards about a quarter inch. The backward bevel helps with this. Slide your fingers back along the surface of the double card so that you're gripping it at the back end between fingers and thumb (Illus. 26). Immediately snap the double card over end for end, moving your right hand forward as you do so. Set the card down so that it projects about an inch-and-a-half beyond the front of the deck (Illus. 27).

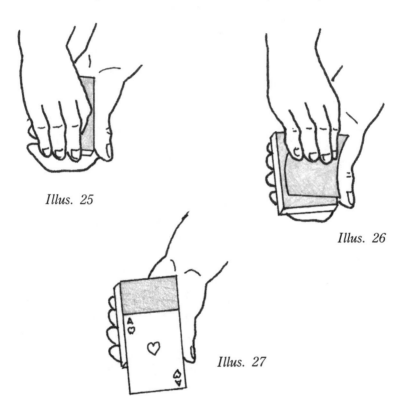

Illus. 25

Illus. 26

Illus. 27

After pausing a few moments, with your palm-up right hand grasp the double card at the right outer side, fingers below and thumb on top (Illus. 28). Lift it off the deck and bring it to the right side of the deck (Illus. 29). With your right fingers beneath, flip the double card face down on top of the deck.

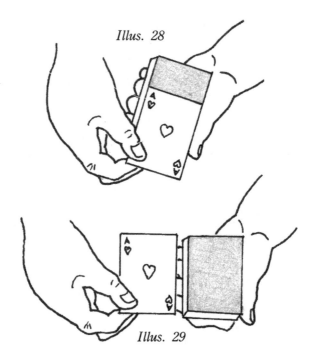

Illus. 28

Illus. 29

Note

It may be difficult at first to separate two cards from the deck with your right thumb. A good way to practise is to perform the double-lift, then deal the top card down. Perform another double-lift; deal the top card down. Continue on through the deck. Eventually, you'll have no trouble at all.

Original Double-Lift

The double-lift I learned as a kid is quite easy and will still do the job for a great many tricks.

As with *Efficient Double-Lift* (p. 32), hold the deck in your left hand with your thumb along the side. Grip the deck with your right hand, as in the previous double-lift (Illus. 25, p. 33). As you chat with the spectators, separate two cards at the rear of the deck with your right thumb. Push these two cards forward about a quarter-inch.

With your right hand, grasp the two cards at the outer end, fingers beneath and thumb on top. This is precisely the same grip shown in Illus. 28 (p. 34), except that, in this instance, the card taken with your right hand is face down. Turn the two cards over end-for-end, and set them down so that they project about an inch beyond the front of the deck.

When ready, grasp the cards at the outer end again, turn them end-for-end, and return them, face down, to the top of the deck.

TRICKS

Tricks with the Double-Lift

Sneaky Slide

Have a card chosen and bring it to the top of the deck. (See *Controlling a Card,* p. 13.) Double-lift the top two, showing the wrong card. Turn the double card face down on top. "There you are, five of clubs," you declare. But the spectator says that you're wrong. You reply, "Oh-oh! I guess I'll have to try real magic."

Take the top card off the deck, grasping its outer edge with your right hand. Pass it through the middle of the deck, from the front end to the back (Illus. 30). Turn the card over, showing that it's magically changed to the chosen one.

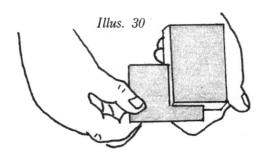

Illus. 30

My Mistake

Have Elizabeth choose a card and show it around. When she returns it to the deck, bring it to second from the top. Simply obtain a little-finger break *one card above* the chosen card after it's returned. Then perform a double-cut (see *Double-Cut,* p. 13).

Explain to the group, "I know you're going to be astonished by this effect, but please hold your applause. When I reveal the chosen card, just marvel in silence so that we all can enjoy the enormous impact."

Perform a double-lift, showing the selected card. Name the card, and then say, "Oh, I'm sorry. I really don't miss that often. I have no idea of what went wrong."

Return the double card to the top of the deck and slide the top card into the middle of the deck.

"Maybe I can work something out." Ask Elizabeth, "What was the name of your card?"

She tells you the name. All the spectators will be happy to inform you that you just stuck the chosen card into the middle of the deck.

"That's all right," you say. "After all, I *am* supposed to be a magician."

Tap the top card and turn it over.

That's Right, You're Wrong!

I developed an improved handling of a trick called "Righting a Wrong," which appeared in Jean Hugard and Fred Braue's *The Royal Road to Card Magic*.

Ask Barney to choose a card. When he returns it, bring it to the top. (See *Controlling a Card*, p. 13.) "Barney," you say, "please think of any number from 5 to 15."

Hand him the deck and ask him to count off that number onto the table. Ask him to *look at* the last card dealt.

"Is that your card?" No. Have him replace the pile on top. "I don't like to criticize, but maybe you didn't count them exactly right."

Pick up the deck. Suppose his chosen number was 11. Deal off ten cards slowly and precisely. "The important thing is to deal the cards *slowly*. Now wouldn't it be amazing if I had your card right here? What was your card?"

Suppose Barney says, "Queen of spades." You double-lift the top two, showing, say, the ten of clubs. "Oh, no, the ten of clubs. I should have guessed. The ten of clubs is a real troublemaker, always popping up when you least want it."

Turn the two face down, and deal the top card (the one chosen) face down onto the table to one side. "So we'll just eliminate that nasty ten of clubs." Place the dealt cards back on top of the deck, commenting, "The trouble is, I dealt the cards *too slowly*. If you deal the cards too slowly, this will never work."

Count off ten cards onto the table, saying, "*Now* it should work." Show the top card. It's the ten of clubs. "Ten of clubs again! Wait a minute . . . what was your card again?" Turn over the card on the table. That's it! Act disgusted. "Just what I thought. The ten of clubs ruined everything."

Am I Blue?

This clever trick was shown to me by Wally Wilson.

A bit of preparation is necessary. For purposes of patter, you must use a red-backed deck. Note the bottom card of that deck. From a blue-backed deck, take a duplicate of that card and place it on the bottom of the red-backed deck.

The situation as you begin: You have, say, a king of hearts second from the bottom of your red-backed deck. On the bottom, you have another king of hearts, which has a blue back.

Fan through the cards, asking Lois to choose one. (Make sure you do not get to the bottom and reveal the blue-backed card.) As she shows the card around, close up the fan. Perform the Hindu Shuffle (p. 19). At about the middle of the deck, stop and ask Lois to replace her card. Hold out the cards in your left hand for the return. Drop the cards in your right hand on top. The blue-backed card is now above the chosen card.

"I wonder if you'd mind blowing on the deck." After she

does so, say, "Blow a little harder, please." If this is evoking amusement, you might ask her to blow even harder. "Oh, my! I think you *blew* too hard." Fan through the deck to the blue-backed card. Cut at that point to bring the blue-backed card to the top. "You *really* blew. In fact, you turned one of the cards blue." Ask, "What was the card you chose?"

Lois tells you. Do the double-lift, demonstrating that the blue-backed card is, in fact, the one she selected. Turn the double card face down and deal the top card (blue-backed) onto the table.

At this point, you have a blue-backed king of hearts face down on the table and the duplicate of that card on the bottom of the deck.

"Let's try it again," you say. You'll now perform the Hindu Shuffle force (p. 20). "Tell me when to stop," you direct Lois. Then commence the Hindu shuffle. When she says stop, show her the bottom card of those in your right hand. Replace these cards on top.

Repeat the business of having her blow on the deck. "Let's see if it worked." Fan through the deck, but this time there's no blue-backed card. Close up the cards and have her blow on the deck again, but once more you fail to find a blue-backed card.

Look puzzled. "I think I know what happened. What's the name of your card?" She names it. "Just as I thought. The king of hearts is a troublemaker, and a really mixed-up card. It can't make up its mind whether it wants to be blue or red." Turn over the card on the table. "See what I mean?"

Pause for a moment. Pick up the blue-backed king of hearts and place it in your pocket, saying, "We'd better get rid of that little rascal."

Note

Perhaps you're wondering, "As I proceed with other tricks, won't people notice that the king of hearts is back in the deck?" They might, and if they comment, you say, "Oh, yes, that little rascal is back." On one occasion, a spectator said to me, "But you put the five of spades in your pocket." My reply was, "Oh, that was a different five of spades," and I went into the next trick.

Yes, it occasionally works well to tell spectators the truth. Since you're a magician, they're unlikely to believe you anyway.

Stay Put!

Ask Lois to cut off about half of the deck. You hold half, she holds half. Say, "Please turn over your top card so we can see what you have." Suppose she turns over the eight of hearts. Say, "Ah, the eight of hearts. You know, the eight of hearts is considered good luck. So you have the eight of hearts. Turn it face down, please, and let's see what I have."

Note that you say the name of her card at least three times.

Double-lift to show your card, announce its name and re-place it face down on top of your packet. "Now we exchange cards," you say. She lifts off her card and places it face down onto your packet, as you lift off your top card and place it face down onto her packet.

Snap your fingers. Double-lift, turning over the top two cards of your packet. Your card has returned. Turn the double card face down. Make sure that Lois does *not* turn over her card. Again she places her top card on your pile as you place yours on top of hers.

Snap your fingers. Your card has returned once more, with the aid of the double-lift. Repeat the procedure again. Once more, do a double-lift, showing that the card has re-turned.

To help you keep track, you perform *four* double-lifts.

After the last double-lift, turn the card face down, saying, "Keep yours. I'll just put mine on your pile." After you put your top card on her pile, say, "Put your hand on top of it so that it can't get away." Snap your fingers and turn over your *top card.* The card's back again!

Ask, "And your card was the eight of hearts, right?" She agrees. Have her turn over her top card. It's the eight of hearts.

Transposition

Ambitious Ace

This is a Nick Trost version of an Al Baker trick.

Openly fan through the deck, removing the ace, two, and three of hearts and placing them on top. It doesn't matter *how* you place them on top, but they must be (from the top down) in this order: ace, two, three.

Hold the cards face down in your left hand in the dealing position. Spread out the top several cards and obtain a break with your little finger beneath the fourth card from the top. With your right hand, turn over the top *three* cards sideways, letting them drop on top of the deck. Comment, "So here we have the ace, two, and three of hearts."

With your palm-down right hand, even up the cards and lift off the top *four.* "Here's the three," you say. Draw the card onto the deck with your left thumb, making sure it's jogged about a half-inch to the right. Bring the remaining cards in your right hand beneath the three of hearts and, with them, flip the three over onto the deck (see Illus. 17, p. 28). Show the two of hearts, saying, "Here's the two." Draw it off with your left thumb, and flip it over in the same manner. As soon as the two of hearts lands face down on the deck, drop the two cards remaining in your right hand on top of it. "And the ace," you say. Turn the ace face down.

The top four cards now are: ace of hearts, any card, two of hearts, three of hearts.

You continue, "Let's see what happens with the ace of

hearts." Take the ace of hearts face down in your right hand.
Push off the top card a bit and slide the ace of hearts under
it. Give the ends of the deck a little riffle. Double-lift the top
two cards, showing that the ace has returned to the top.
Turn the two cards face down. Lift off the top card and place
it on the bottom.

Now you're done with sleight of hand; the other miracles
occur automatically.

As you turn the ace of hearts face down, comment, "Just
as I thought. These three cards are extremely ambitious.
They always want to be on top. We'll get rid of the ace." At
this point, place the top card on the bottom.

Now on top are the ace of hearts, two of hearts, and three
of hearts. Say, "Let's see what happens with the two of
hearts." Place the top card second from the top. Give the
deck a little riffle. Turn over the top card, showing that the
two of hearts has returned to the top. (Make sure you turn
it over in exactly the same manner as you previously performed the double-lift.) "Yes, the two is also very ambitious." Turn the two of hearts face down, take it from the
deck, and place it on the bottom.

Deal with the three of hearts exactly as you dealt with the
two of hearts, placing it on the bottom after you turn it face
down.

"Yes, the two of hearts and the three of hearts really like
being on top. But the most ambitious of all is . . . the ace of
hearts." Turn the top card over, showing that the ace of
hearts has returned. Again, *make sure you turn it over exactly
as you turned the cards over with the double-lift.*

One in Four

This trick is quite similar to the previous trick in its basic principle. But its *effect* is quite different. Roy Walton combined tricks by Al Baker and Dai Vernon; my only contribution is to add a slightly different handling.

Remove from the deck the four, three, two and ace of any suit. (Let's assume that you're using diamonds.) First find the four and place it face up on the table. On top of this place the face-up three, followed by the two and the ace.

Ask Jeanine to choose a card and show it around. When she returns it to the deck, bring it to the top. (See *Controlling a Card,* p. 13.)

Hold the deck in the dealing position in your left hand. Pick up the four face-up cards from the table and drop them face up on top of the deck. Spread them out, along with another card or two. Say, "Here we have the ace, two, three, and four of diamonds." As you close up the four diamonds with your palm-up right hand, get a break with your left little finger below the fifth card. Immediately, turn your right hand palm down and lift off the packet of five cards, fingers at the outer end, thumb at the inner end. The top, face-up card of the packet is the ace of diamonds, followed by the other three diamonds in order. On the bottom of the packet is the face-down chosen card.

"It's important that you remember the order of the cards," you say. "First, we have the ace." You now turn over the ace lengthwise and add it to the bottom of the packet. Here's precisely how: Move the packet in your right hand over the deck and hold down the ace with your left thumb as you move the rest of the packet to the right, drawing off the ace. The ace should extend over the right side of the deck about half its width (Illus. 31). From below, lift the packet in your right hand so that its left edge flips the ace over sideways. *Leave your left thumb in place, so that the ace falls on it.* Bring your

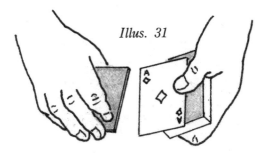

Illus. 31

right hand over the face-down ace, so that the ace is added to the bottom of the packet.

Call attention to the two of diamonds, saying, "And here we have the two." In the same way as you did the ace, turn the two of diamonds face down and add it to the bottom of the packet.

In exactly the same way, show the three and then the four. Drop the packet on top of the deck.

On top of the deck is the chosen card, followed by the ace, two, three, and four of diamonds.

Say to Jeanine, "I'd like you to choose one of the four cards—ace, two, three, or four. In fact, think of one, and then change your mind. I want you to have complete freedom of choice." She chooses one of the cards.

Suppose the ace is chosen. Deal the top card face down onto the table, saying, "All right, there's the ace. Now let's see how the two behaves." Without showing the top card, place it second from the top. Tap the top card and then turn it over. Apparently the two has returned to the top. Place the two *face up* next to the card on the table.

"Let's check the three." Place the top card second from the top. Tap the top card and turn it over. The three has returned. Deal it face up next to the two.

"And the four?" Again, place the top card second from the

top. Tap the top card and turn it over, showing that the four has returned. Deal it face up to the right of the three.

Gesture towards the table. "So we have ace, two, three, four of diamonds. And you chose the ace. What's the name of your card?" The spectator names it. Turn over the face-down card. Success!

Suppose the spectator chooses two, three, or four. In each instance, the chosen number is simply dealt face down onto the table; each of the others is placed second from the top, brought back to the top, turned face up, and dealt face up onto the table.

Let's suppose Jeanine chooses three, for instance. "Fine," you say. "Let's see how the ace behaves." Place the top card second from the top. Tap the top card, showing that the ace has returned. Place the ace on the table face up.

Place the top card second from the top, saying, "Let's see what the two does." Tap the top card. Sure enough, the two has returned to the top. Deal it face up to the right of the ace. Deal the next card face down to the right of the other two cards, saying, "Here's your three."

Once more place the top card second from the top, saying, "Let's see what the four does." Tap the top card; the four has returned to the top. Deal it face up to the right of the other three cards.

In all instances, you finally ask the name of the chosen card and then turn it face up.

Travelling Hearts

In concept, *Travelling Hearts* is similar to the preceding trick.

The original of this trick, which was shown to me by Bob Stencel, required a bottom deal. I changed the trick to suit my abilities.

Look through the deck so that spectators can't see the faces. Cut the ace of spades to the top. Then toss out these hearts, in any order, face up onto the table: ace, two, three, four, five, six.

Set down the deck and put the cards in order, the ace being at the face of the face-up packet and the six at the bottom. As you do so, say, "Try to remember what these cards are. For whatever reason, some people don't pay attention; all they can think of is the ace of spades. *Please . . .* these are hearts!"

As you speak, pick up the deck and hold it in your left hand in the dealing position. With your right hand, pick up the packet of hearts and place it face up on top of the deck. You'll now add a card to the packet, exactly as described in the previous trick. Spread out the hearts, displaying them. As you do so, casually spread out a few additional cards. As you close up the cards with your palm-up right hand, get a slight break with your left little finger under the seventh card. Turn your right hand palm down and lift off all seven cards with your right hand, fingers at the outer end, thumb at the inner end. Set the rest of the deck aside.

You're now holding the six hearts face up, with the ace of spades face down on the bottom. Take the packet in your left hand.

Say, "Try to remember these cards . . . *and* their order." Take the ace of hearts in your right hand, saying its name. Turn the card face down and place it face down on the bottom of the packet. With your right hand, turn the packet over, showing the ace on the bottom. Repeat, "Ace of hearts."

Perform the exact same procedure with the two of hearts. For the rest, you simply announce the name of the card, turn it over, and place it on the bottom. The last card you place on the bottom is, of course, the six of hearts. Casually drop the packet on top of the deck.

The top six cards of the deck are, from the top: ace of spades, ace of hearts, two of hearts, three of hearts, four of hearts, and five of hearts.

Deal the top six cards into a row on the table. As you place the cards down, say, "Ace, two, three, four, five, six."

Pause. "Now watch this. We exchange the ace and the two." Change the places of the first two cards. Snap your fingers. Turn over the first card in the row. "The ace of hearts returns. Let's try the two."

Leaving the ace face up, do the same exchange with the second and third cards. Snap your fingers. "The two is back. Let's try the three."

Leave the two face up.

Perform the same maneuver with the third card, the fourth card, and the fifth card. At this point, you have face up on the table the ace, two, three, four, and five of hearts, along with the face-down ace of spades.

"So we have one card left. And, of course, we all know what it is." Pause. "Well, what is it?"

Most of the time, the answer will be, "The six of hearts."

Shake your head. Turn the ace of spades over. "Just as I say, some people just don't pay attention."

Once in a while, a spectator will guess the ace of spades. "Right you are!" you say. "At least *some* people pay attention."

Joker Helps

Before I explain this Jack Avis transposition trick, I'll teach you a sleight called *Mexican Turnover*. It's a quite useful method for exchanging two cards.

Place a card face down on the table. Take another card

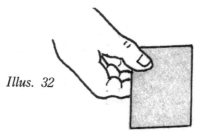

Illus. 32

face down in your right hand, holding it at the lower right corner with your thumb on top and your first two fingers beneath (Illus. 32). The third and fourth fingers of your right hand are curled into your palm. Presumably, you'll turn over the card on the table with the card in your hand.

Place your left first finger on the lower left corner of the card on the table, tilting the opposite side up slightly. Slide

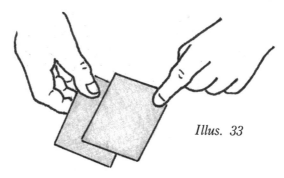

Illus. 33

the card in your hand under the right side of the table card, so that the bottom card extends a little less than an inch above the upper card (Illus. 33). Tilt both hands counterclockwise slightly. As you do so, your right thumb and second finger grip the *upper* card. This card is lifted several inches at about a 45° angle. In that same motion, your right first finger flips the lower card face up—sideways. (Naturally, as you perform the flipping action, your left hand moves to the left, releasing the hold of its first finger on the card which was originally on the table.) The sleight should be performed at medium speed; *don't rush it!*

You might practise by alternately performing a legitimate turnover and *Mexican Turnover.*

Now, the trick. Lay three cards out on the table, left to right: an ace, a joker, and a three. Emphasize the position of the ace and the three. Pick up the face-up joker and apparently turn the three face down. Actually, perform *Mexican Turnover.* Make sure that no one sees that the face-down three is in your right hand as you continue moving the card to the left and drop it face down on the face-up ace.

Pick up the two cards and hold them in the dealer's grip in your left hand. The three is face down on top; the ace is face up on the bottom. Turn over your left hand and push the cards through your hand with your left thumb (Illus. 34). Take them at the outer end with your right hand. Now the

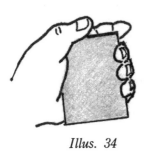

Illus. 34

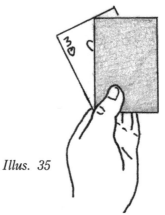

Illus. 35

ace is on top face down and the three is on the bottom face up. Turn your left hand palm up and replace the two cards there. Fan the two cards, revealing the three (Illus. 35).

Set aside the face-up three. Now exchange the face-down ace with the face-down joker on the table, using *Mexican Turnover*. The ace and the three have changed places. Casually toss the joker face up onto the table.

Join the Knavery

Fan through the deck, faces towards yourself. Make no attempt at concealment as you cut the queen of diamonds to the top. Place the queen of spades on top of that. So, the second card from the top of the deck is the queen of diamonds; the top card is the queen of spades. Toss the two black jacks and the queen of hearts face up onto the table.

As you do the above, say, "I'd like to tell you a tale of two loving sisters, who happened to be queens, and another queen, who happened to be an evil witch."

You now do half of a legitimate one-finger cut, described in detail at the beginning of *Don't Pass It Up,* p. 15. Your left first finger is pointed upwards behind the deck. In this instance, however, you revolve about *two-thirds* of the cards from the top of the deck so that they fall into your left hand. Place the part remaining in your right hand on the table to your left. "Here we have the castle in which one of the red queens lived." Touch the queen of hearts, which is face up on the table. "This queen, in fact. One day, two evil knaves came to the castle and kidnapped the queen and took her into the forest. Once there, they blindfolded her." Say to Oliver, a willing spectator, "To show that, please put her face down between the two evil knaves." He makes a sandwich of the three cards, the queen of hearts being face down between the two face-up jacks.

" 'What are you going to do to me?' asked the queen.

" 'When evening comes, we'll leave you to be eaten by wild beasts.'

" 'But besides you two, there are no wild beasts in this forest.'

" 'Then when evening comes, we'll kill you.'

" 'That's more like it,' said the queen, who was something of a perfectionist.

"And who was responsible for the kidnapping? This wicked witch, who also happened to be a queen—the queen of spades."

With the packet in your hand, now perform *Drop Sleight,* exactly as described on page 28. During the previous patter, you do the necessary preparation of letting the bottom card drop slightly and holding a break with your right thumb between this card and the rest of the packet. Then you proceed with half of a one-finger cut, and the actual sleight. As you say, "—the queen of spades," turn the top card of the left-hand packet over, using the left edge of the cards in your right hand. It is, of course, the queen of spades. Continue your patter as you complete the sleight, replacing the queen of spades with an indifferent card.

"She didn't have a castle, so she had the red queen kidnapped and took over her castle."

Place the cards in your right hand on the table, slightly to the right. With your right hand take off the top card of those in your left hand and place it on top of the pile on the left. Apparently this card is the queen of spades.

As you proceed with the patter, place the cards in your left hand on top of those you just set on the table. Pick up the entire packet and hold it in your left hand.

The situation: On top of the packet you're holding is the queen of spades. Below it is the queen of diamonds.

"How wicked was she? Why, she'd talk with her mouth full of food. She'd cry when she didn't get her own way. And, worst of all, she'd torture her subjects by singing off-key until they begged for mercy.

"Now, with all this talk, I'll bet some of you can't remember which red queen we have in the forest. Is it the diamond queen or her sister, the heart queen?"

Pick up the three cards on the table and hold them fanned in your right hand. Meanwhile, push off the top card of the packet slightly and draw it back, getting a left little-finger break beneath it. Close up the three-card fan onto the packet, adding the additional card to the bottom of the group. Immediately lift off all four cards with your palm-down right hand, fingers at the outer end and thumb at the inner end.

"Can you remember which one was kidnapped? Was it the heart queen or the diamond queen?" Whatever the answer, with your left thumb draw the top face-up jack onto the packet. Thumb it face up onto the table. With your left thumb, draw the face-down queen of hearts onto the packet, letting it hang over the right side of the packet about half its width.

Flip it over with the left side of the double card in your right hand, again letting it hang over about half its width.

"Ah, it's the queen of hearts—*not* her wonderful sister, the queen of diamonds."

With the right side of the double card, flip the queen of hearts face down, even with the top of the packet. With the same motion, drop the double card on top. Immediately fan off the top two cards, take them in your right hand, and place them on the jack on the table. The three should be spread out, forming a fan.

The queen of spades is now face down between the two face-up jacks, and the queen of hearts is on top of the packet in your hand. The second card from the top is the queen of diamonds. Do a double-lift, showing the queen of diamonds. Ask, "How many of you thought it was really the queen of diamonds?" Turn the double card face down. "Wrong, wrong, wrong!" Hold the packet from above in your right hand. Draw off the top card (the presumed queen of diamonds) with your *left* hand. "The diamond queen left her castle . . ." Move your right hand up and down slightly, indicating that the packet there is the castle in question. Place the card which is in your left hand on top of the packet on your left. ". . . and went to the wicked queen to beg for her sister's life."

Place the packet which is in your right hand down to your right.

" 'Please spare my sister's life!' she begged.

" 'Nuts to you with shells on,' said the evil queen.

" 'Then you'll be sorry,' said the diamond queen.

" 'Why should I be sorry? I'm an evil witch and I have evil witch powers.'

"And the diamond queen said, 'But I'm a good witch, and I have good witch powers—which are way stronger than evil witch powers. And now, I'll sing a magic spell (sing) When you wish upon a star, Makes no . . . Wait a minute

. . . wrong movie. I've got it . . . (sing) Bibbety, bobbety, bibbety, bobbety, bibbety, bobbety boo.' And with that, both castles shook a little."

Casually show that both hands are empty. Reach out and simultaneously give each pile a little riffle.

"Instantly . . . the diamond queen was back in her castle." Turn over the top card of the pile on the right, leaving it face up on top. "And . . ." Turn over the top card of the other pile. ". . . the heart queen was back in her castle." Pause. During the following, spread the two jacks aside and turn over the queen of spades: "And the evil queen was alone in the forest with the two nasty knaves!" Before the audience has a chance to react, immediately say, "Soooo . . . they all lived happily ever after."

Quite Quaint Queens

This trick requires very little work but accomplishes an extraordinary result. This gem is the brainchild of Alan Brown.

Since you already have most of the cards you need on the table from the previous trick, you can continue the story by doing this trick. You may, however, prefer to perform this trick by itself.

Take out the jacks from the deck. Place the two red jacks, face up and fanned out, upon the table to the left; place the two black jacks, face up and fanned out, upon the table to the right. Remove the queen of spades and queen of hearts from the deck and place them near you, face up upon the table.

"The black jacks," you say, "are evil knaves. They work for this evil queen." Tap the queen of spades.

"The red jacks, however, are nice guys. They work for this very good queen." Tap the queen of hearts.

"One day, the evil queen had the good queen kidnapped by her evil knaves." Place the queen of hearts face up between the two face-up black jacks, so that the lady becomes the middle card of the three-card fan. "They took her into the forest and blindfolded her." Ask Arnold to turn the queen of hearts face down, indicating that the queen's blindfolded. So the three-card fan now consists of the face-down queen of hearts surrounded by the two face-up black jacks.

Pick up the queen of spades. "While this was going on, the evil queen held the good guys prisoner with her crossbow." Place the queen of spades *face up* between the two red jacks, so that the three cards form a fan on the table.

"Why did the evil queen do this? Because she wanted this castle for herself." As you say "this castle," hold out the deck, showing that it represents the castle. "So the evil queen of spades went inside the castle with the two nice guys, the red jacks." (This is to implant the precise position in the minds of the spectators.)

Hold the deck in the dealing position in your left hand. Pick up the fan of the red jacks and the queen of spades. Retaining their order (jacks on the outside), turn the three face down, and place them on top of the deck. As you close up the face-down trio, get a break with your right thumb below the top card. Double-undercut the deck, bringing the top card to the bottom. (See *Double-Cut,* p. 13.) "There go the red jacks and the evil queen of spades."

Gesture towards the remaining trio on the table. "The evil knaves were really stupid, and they forgot why they'd kidnapped the good queen of hearts. So they returned to the castle."

With your right hand, reach over to pick up the top black jack. As you do so, push off the top card of the deck slightly with your left thumb. Draw the card back on top of the deck, getting a tiny break beneath it with the tip of your left little finger. Place the black jack *face up* on top of the deck. "One evil knave entered the castle." Pick up the queen of hearts and place it face down on top of the deck. "When the good queen of hearts got into the castle, she slammed the door, and ran away."

You now have the queen of hearts on top, and the card below it is a black jack. Below the third card from the top, you have a little-finger break. Double-undercut the deck, bringing the top three cards to the bottom.

All the dirty work is done.

"The other evil knave finally managed to get the door open . . ." Pick up the other black jack and place it face up on top. ". . . and he immediately began searching for the queen of hearts." Give the cards a legitimate cut in the middle. Then cut off an additional small packet (ten cards or so) and complete the cut.

Snap the ends of the cards. "Now let's see what happened." Fan through the cards to the face-up black jacks and the face-down card between them. "The evil knaves finally found the queen in the dark. So they dragged her out of the castle and took her into the forest." Remove the three cards together from the deck and place the three on the table. Close up the deck.

"But they made one little mistake. They had the wrong queen." Turn the middle card of the three over, showing that it's the queen of spades.

"And what about the queen of hearts?" Turn the deck face up and fan through so that all can see. "Let's find those nice guys, the red jacks. There they are. And right between them, we have the good queen of hearts . . . just as it should be."

Discoveries

Logical Progression

Here, I've modified a John Scarne trick.

Ask Hervé to select a card. When he returns it, bring it to the top. (See *Controlling a Card,* p. 13.)

Tell Hervé, "Very slowly, I'm going to give you a number progression. I'd like you to stop me whenever you wish." Slowly recite these numbers: 1, 2, 4, 8, 16, 32. If he hasn't stopped you by the time you hit 32, tell him, "Let's start again," and repeat the numbers.

In the unlikely event that Hervé stops you at 1 or 2, say, with feigned exasperation, "Give me a chance . . . *please!*" Any other number is just fine.

Hand Hervé the pack. "You've chosen the number 16" (or whatever). "Please count that many cards off the deck into a pile."

Then he is to pick up the pile he counted off. "Deal the top card onto the table, Hervé, and then put the next card on the bottom of the pile. The next one on the table, and the next one on the bottom." He is to continue dealing this way until he holds only one card. Ask Hervé to name his card and then turn over the one he is holding. You did it again!

This down-under fashion of dealing is referred to as "the Australian shuffle." Your group may not have heard the gag, so feel free to use it when giving Hervé his instructions.

Magnificent Seven

Stewart Judah originated this trick, in which a chosen card appears at a "freely chosen" number from the top.

Force a card on a spectator. (See *Forces,* p. 23.) After he returns the card to the deck, have him shuffle the cards. Take the cards back and fan through them, faces towards yourself.

"I doubt that I can find your card, but maybe you'll have better luck." Cut the deck, bringing a seven to the bottom. Take it off the deck and, without showing its face, toss it face down on the table. Follow the same cutting procedure, bringing to the bottom any card other than a seven or the chosen card. Place this to the right of the seven. Fan through to another seven; cut this to the bottom and place it face down on the table to the right of the other two cards. An indifferent card goes face down to the right of these. Continue this procedure until you have this layout on the table (from your point of view):

7 X 7 X 7 X

In selecting the last card to place down, fan through to the chosen card. Count it as "one" and continue counting to yourself as you spread the cards. Cut the pack so that card number seven becomes the top card. The chosen card is now the seventh card from the top of the deck. Take the bottom card and place it face down to the right of the others. (In the unlikely event that this card happens to be the fourth seven, simply shake your head and stick it into the middle of the deck. Take the new bottom card and place it to the right of the others.)

If a die is handy, have the spectator roll it out. If not, have him choose a number from 1 to 6. (Or mentally roll a die.) Now count to that number in your layout, and you'll land on a seven!

If the number 1 is chosen, start at the left and count, "One." Turn the card over, saying, "A seven." Casually turn over the next card to the right, demonstrating that it's *not* a seven.

If 2 is chosen, count from the *right*. Again a seven. Turn over the cards on both sides; neither is a seven.

If 3 is chosen, count from the left. If 4 is chosen, count from the right. If 5 is chosen, count from the left. In all instances, turn over the cards on both sides.

If 6 is chosen, count from the right, turn over the seven, and show that the card to the right of it isn't a seven.

"So, by chance, you've selected a seven." Deal off seven cards from the top into a pile, counting aloud. Gather up the cards in your layout and casually shuffle them into the deck, saying, "There's no doubt that you had complete freedom of choice, so the question is: 'Were you lucky or not?' What's

the name of your card?" The spectator names it. Have him
turn over the card himself. He was *very* lucky.

Instant Location

It's surprisingly easy to riffle the cards from hand to hand. If
you wish to try it, I recommend that you practise over a table
or bed; it makes picking the cards up much easier.

First, I'll explain how to do the hand-to-hand riffle. Then
I'll explain a cute trick you can do with it.

Hold the cards at the ends in your palm-down right hand.
Your left hand is held palm up to catch the cards. Move your
right fingers and thumb together, making the cards bulge
upwards in the middle (Illus. 36). As you keep bending, cards

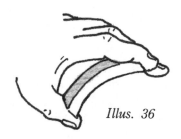

Illus. 36

will individually slip off the bottom of the pack and fall into
your left hand.

As you've perhaps already discovered, it's best to start
with your left hand only a few inches below the deck. As you
become more skilled, you can expand the distance. For the
purpose of the trick, however, the distance need not be
great.

Stand with your right side towards the spectators. The
deck is held in the riffling position in your right hand, with the
faces of the cards towards the spectators. Riffle to your left
hand a substantial number of cards. Call attention to the card
on the face of the group in your left hand. Slap the cards in

your right hand onto those in your left hand. Even up the deck and then take it into your right hand. Once more riffle off a bunch of cards and call attention to the card which faces the spectators. Do this a few more times, explaining, "You'll notice that it's virtually impossible for me to stop at the same card twice. So I'll look away while you take a look at the next card I stop at."

Riffle all the cards except the bottom one into your left hand. (Try this a few times; you'll be quite startled at how easy it is.) "See the card?" Immediately slap the bottom card onto the face of those in your left hand. Even up the cards and turn the deck face down. The "chosen" card is now second from the bottom, at your disposal.

Clearly, there are dozens of ways to finish the trick. I like doing it this way: I carefully even up all the cards and display the deck so that everyone can see that there are no breaks of any kind. I turn the deck face up in my left hand in the dealing position. Then I bring both hands behind my back simultaneously. I push off the bottom card with my left thumb, and pull off the second card from the bottom (the one selected) with my right thumb. I quickly bring both hands forward, displaying the selection in my right hand. In the process, I pull back the bottom card so that it's even with the rest of the deck.

The entire action takes about a second.

Notes
The move can also be used as a force. You need to know the second card from the bottom. An easy way is to sight the bottom card and then shuffle it to the top in an overhand shuffle. Do another overhand shuffle. With the first move of the shuffle, squeeze slightly with your left thumb and fingers, thus retaining the top and bottom cards. Shuffle off the rest of the deck. The card you peeked at is now second from the bottom.

In exactly the way described above, show that you cannot stop at the same card twice. Avert your head and ask a spectator to note the card you stop at. When you riffle, retain only the bottom card. The spectator sees the force card. Slap the one card onto those riffled off. You can now read the spectator's mind or proceed with any other trick in which a force is necessary.

If you're performing the hand-to-hand riffle as a flourish, start with your hands quite close together. As you begin the riffle, don't move your left hand, but bring your right hand up about a foot. By the time your right hand has reached this point, about half the deck should have been riffled off. *Immediately* and rapidly bring your hands together; this tends to keep the cards from scattering. Eventually, you may be able to expand the distance.

Something Old

It has to be more than a century since a gambler actually thought he could get away with stacking cards using this peculiar method. But while the method isn't suitable for stacking cards, it's ideal for a card trick.

Before you start, place four cards of the same value on the bottom of the deck. Let's assume you use the four sevens. Using the Hindu shuffle, do the preparation for the standard force. (See *Standard Force,* p. 23.) Now perform the force; you're almost certain to succeed, for you are to force any one of the sevens.

Before the spectator chooses one of the sevens, however, provide these instructions: "I'd like you to select one of these cards, but please don't look at it. Simply draw it from the deck and place it face down on the table."

After the card is taken, get a break with your left little finger beneath the remaining three sevens. Bring the sevens to the bottom with the double-cut. (See *Double-Cut,* p. 13.)

You now have a seven face down on the table and three

sevens on the bottom of the deck, and you're ready to perform the stacking maneuver I mentioned earlier.

Turn so that your left side is towards the onlookers. Hold the deck in the overhand shuffle position in your left hand. Spectators, of course, are looking at the back of the top card.

Say to your assistant, "Please say stop whenever you wish." You proceed to perform a special version of the overhand shuffle. With the first movement, lift up with your right hand all the cards except the top card and the bottom card. This is done by *squeezing* the top and bottom cards together with the left fingers and thumb as you lift the others with your right hand. *Immediately,* with your left thumb, draw off the top card onto these two. Continue rapidly drawing off single cards until the spectator says stop. Place the cards in your left hand face down onto the table, making sure no one sees the bottom card.

Again ask the spectator to say stop as you shuffle. Go through the same procedure. With the first move of the shuffle, draw off the top and bottom cards, and then shuffle off cards one at a time. When the spectator says stop, place the pile in your left hand to the right of the first pile.

Have your assistant say stop once more, as you go through the shuffle. This pile is placed to the right of the other two.

Set the rest of the deck aside.

"Nearly every day we hear about some startling coincidence. Let's see if coincidence will operate here. Please turn over the card you selected."

The spectator obliges.

"Ah, a seven. And let's see what these other cards are."

Turn over the three piles, showing that each has a seven at the bottom.

Queen of India

The key move is derived from a Steve Beam trick which required some preparation. This uses the same move in an impromptu trick.

Remove from the deck the ace of clubs, ace of spades, king of diamonds, king of hearts, and the queen of diamonds, tossing them face up on the table. Pick up the queen of diamonds. "Here we have one of the most famous diamonds in the world, 'The Queen of India.' " Drop the queen face down onto the table.

"And where you have big diamonds, you have thieves. In fact, here we have two kings of thieves—members of the notorious Red Gang." Pick up the two red kings, displaying them. Drop them as a pair face down onto the table. "But we also have two ace detectives—Sam Spade and Clem Club." Display the black aces and drop them face down as a pair onto the table.

Pick up the deck. "Here we have the museum where the Queen of India will be put on display. But before she's put on display, we'd better bring in the detectives." Pick up the aces, show them, and drop them face down on top of the deck. Lift the top ace with your right thumb and give the cards a double-cut (see *Double-Cut,* p. 13), bringing one ace to the bottom and the other to the top.

"But those nasty thieves managed to sneak into the museum . . ." Display the red kings and drop them face down on top of the deck. As you lift the top card with your right thumb and perform a double-cut, continue, ". . . where they cleverly hid themselves."

The top and bottom cards are red kings; the second card from the top and the second card from the bottom are black aces. Make sure you don't flash the bottom card.

Pick up the queen of diamonds and hand it face down to a spectator. "Now we'd better put the Queen of India on display. Would you put the diamond into the museum? Just stick the card in about halfway." She sticks the face-down card into the deck about halfway.

Laughingly say, "Wait a minute. The Queen of India is supposed to be on display. We can't see her."

Now perform the sleight I mentioned. Fan the cards into your right hand until you come to the face-down queen. With your right hand, lift off all the cards above the queen. Turn your right hand palm down. The cards it's holding are now face up (Illus. 37). Move your right hand to the outer

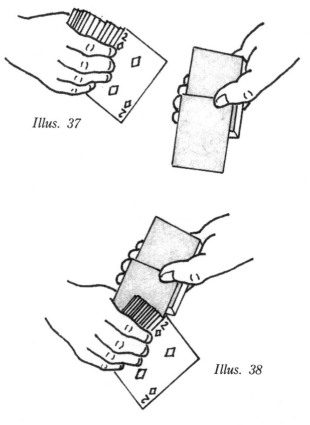

Illus. 37

Illus. 38

edge of the deck. With your right thumb, pick off the protruding face-down queen (Illus. 38). Turn over your right hand so that it's palm up again. You're now holding a face-down packet in your palm-up right hand, with your right thumb gripping the face-up queen (Illus. 39).

Place the cards in your left hand on top of those in your right hand so that they're even with the main packet in your right hand. The queen is now face up as it sticks out from the middle. "That's better." Leaving the deck exactly as it is, set it down on the table.

"There we have the Queen of India on display. And we have the ace detectives wandering around the museum. But the kings of thieves are very resourceful."

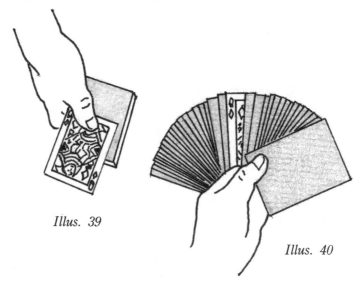

Illus. 39

Illus. 40

Pick up the deck and fan down to the face-up queen. Spread out the cards on each side and hold the deck in your left hand (Illus. 40). On each side of the queen is a red king. Turn them both face up in place. "Ah, the kings of thieves indeed managed to capture the Queen of India." Pause. "But it didn't do them much good . . ." Turn over in place the cards on each side of the red kings, the black aces. ". . . because the ace detectives captured them."

Four Aces

Sneaky Aces

This trick was shown to me by Wally Wilson, who felt it was the invention of Harry Lorayne.

Unknown to the spectators, you have the four aces on top of the deck. False-shuffle the cards, leaving the aces on top. Set the deck on the table. Ask Myra to cut the deck in half, and then to cut each half in half.

There are now four piles on the table. Make sure you keep track of which pile has the aces on top. Pick up that pile.

Say to Myra, "Let's see how you did." One by one, take the top card of each of the other piles and place it face down on top of the packet in your hand.

"We have to build suspense here. You cut to four cards." Count aloud, as you deal off the four top cards onto the table, one on top of the other. Pick up the four and place them back onto the packet, getting a break beneath them with your left little finger.

You should be holding the packet quite close to the pile which is on the table to the right. Turn over the top card and set it squarely on the packet. "Ah, an ace!"

With your palm-down right hand grip the top four cards, fingers at the front, thumb at the back. Lift off the four cards and place them on top of the pile which is on the right on the table. Apparently, you've placed only the ace on the pile.

Turn over the next card on top of the deck. "Another ace!" In precisely the same way as you gripped the four-card pile, grip the ace and place it face up on top of one of the other piles.

Do the same with the next ace. Finally, turn over the top card of the deck. Evidently, Myra has cut to all four aces.

Gaze at her in wonder and say, "My, I'd hate to play cards with you!"

Grand Illusion

Fr. Cyprian is credited with the subtle move used in this trick.

Start with two aces on top of the deck and two on the bottom. (You might do this: After performing a four-ace trick, make sure the four aces are together somewhere in the deck. Perform a few more tricks. Then casually fan through the deck and cut between the aces, bringing two to the top and two to the bottom.) Give the deck a riffle shuffle, keeping two aces on top and two on the bottom. Set the deck on the table.

Joe's a good sport, so ask him to help out. "Joe, would you please cut the deck in half."

After he does, pick up the packet with the aces on top and give it a false shuffle, retaining the aces on top. (See *Controlling a Group of Cards,* p. 22.) Set the pile down.

Pick up the other packet and shuffle the bottom two aces to the top. (See *Bringing the Bottom Card to the Top,* p. 21.) Set this packet down near you, at a diagonal from the other packet. The positions of the two halves on the table:

A
    B

Cards will be cut from these packets and placed on the table. Packets will then be at these positions:

A   C
D   B

This is how it comes about: Have Joe cut off some cards from the packet at A. Point to position D and have him place the cards there. Have him cut off some cards from the packet at B and have him place these at position C.

The situation: Two aces are on top of the packet at position D and two aces are on top of the packet at position C.

Say, "Joe, I wonder how well you did."

Simultaneously grasp the top card at position C with your right hand and the top card at position D with your left hand. Grasp the card at position C at the *far end,* and the card at position D at the *near end.* Turn these aces face up at the same time. Place the ace from position C face up on top of the packet at B; place the ace from position D face up on top of the packet at A.

Again you'll grasp the top card at position C with your right hand and the top card at position D with your left hand. This time, however, you grasp the card at position C at the *near end* and the card at position D at the *far end.* Simultaneously turn these aces face up and place them on the piles from which you just lifted them.

This entire business of turning over the aces takes but a few seconds. If you follow with the cards, you'll see how simple it actually is. The illusion is that the top card of each packet was an ace.

"Good job, Joe! You cut the aces."

Royal Following

The basic trick was invented by Gianni (Roxy) Pasqua. I've eliminated some of the more difficult maneuvers. A setup is required, so this should be your first trick. Here's the way to do the setup: Take from the deck the tens, jacks, queens, kings, and aces. Place three tens face down on the table. Place *face up* on top of these (in order) the four aces, the four kings, the four queens, and the four jacks. Put the rest of the deck (except for the fourth ten) face up on top of these. Place the fourth ten on the bottom of the deck.

From the top down, here's the setup: three tens reversed, four aces, four kings, four queens, and four jacks, followed by the rest of the deck, the bottom card being the fourth ten. Place the deck in the card case so that the face-up deck will face the side where the flap tucks in.

Remove the deck from the case face up, taking care not to reveal the reversed tens. Fan through the cards until you come to the first jack. Cut off all the cards above the first jack, turn them over, and set them face down on the table. The bottom card of this pile is a ten.

Fan off the four face-up jacks, taking them in your right hand. Say, "We start with the four jacks." Turn your right hand palm down and place the jacks face down behind the other cards (Illus. 41). "Then come the four queens." Repeat the operation with the queens. Do the same with the

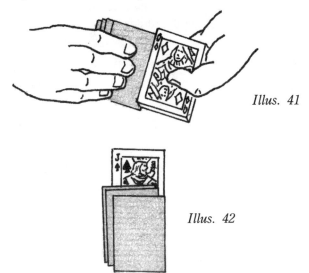

Illus. 41

Illus. 42

four kings and the four aces. You now have a face-down pile in your left hand. The top three cards are tens, followed by the jacks, queens, kings, and aces. Place the pile on top of the deck and pick up the deck.

"First the jacks." Deal the first three cards, one at a time, face down on the table. Turn the fourth card face up and slide it beneath the other three, but leave half its length exposed (Illus. 42). As you deal out the four cards, say, "One, two, three, four jacks."

Repeat the operation with the queens, dealing the cards to the right of your first pile. Below the first pile, deal the kings in the same manner. To the right of this, deal the aces. You'll have formed a sort of square with the four piles.

Fan out the top several cards, saying, "Now you're going to have to choose one of these cards." As you close up the cards, get a little-finger break below the third card from the top. Take the deck from above into your right hand, transferring the break to your right thumb. Say, "We'll check out two cards." Lift off about half the packet with your right hand, keeping the thumb break. Dig your left thumb beneath the packet your left hand is holding and flip this packet over. Slide this packet on top of the cards in your right hand (Illus. 43). You'll be showing the fourth ten, the original bottom

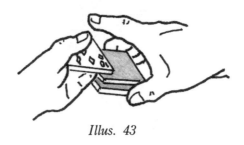

Illus. 43

card. "Which would you prefer," you ask, "the ten . . ." With the left hand, take away all the cards below the thumb break and hold these a bit to the left of your right hand. Dig your left thumb beneath this packet and flip this packet over, revealing another face-up card. Let's say it's a five. Be sure your two hands are separated enough so that the spectator can see both cards clearly. ". . . or the five?" If he chooses the ten, say, "Fine." Place the cards in your right hand on top of those in your left hand. Deal off the face-up ten to one side. Turn the deck face down and set it to the right of your four piles. The three aces are now face up in the center. (If he chooses the other card, say sardonically, "Oh, swell! So I get stuck with the ten." Proceed exactly as above. Either way, of course, the ten is used.)

"Sometimes, if all goes well, the high cards in the deck will play follow-the-leader. Let's see if they're in the mood." Exchange the face-up jack with the face-up queen. Snap your fingers or make a magical gesture. Turn up the cards where the jack now resides; they're all jacks.

Exchange the face-up queen and the face-up king. Show that the queens are now all together. Exchange the face-up ace with the face-up king. The kings have also followed the leader.

"Now let's try the selected card," you say, picking up the face-up ten from the table with your right hand. With your left hand, pick up the face-up ace and place it, face up and crosswise, on top of the deck. Place the ten where the ace formerly resided. Snap your fingers and show that the tens are now all together.

"A face-up ace," you say, slapping the top of the deck with it. Toss the ace aside. Spread out the deck, showing that the other three aces are face up in the middle.

Unexpected Reversal

Rhett Bryson invented this subtle reversal trick. I devised a variation using the aces. This trick can serve as an excellent introduction to a series of four-ace tricks.

Remove the aces from the deck, tossing them face up onto

the table. Pick up the two red aces and place them face up on top of the deck. On top of them place the two black aces face down. Say, "The red aces are face up, and the black aces are face down."

Cut the deck, bringing the aces to the middle. Fan through the cards to the red aces. "See? The red aces are reversed. It's easy to remember which cards are reversed since 're-versed' and 'red' both begin with the same letter."

While chatting, with the tips of your right fingers push the two black aces to the left and get a break with your left little finger above them. In virtually the same movement, slide all the cards above them to the left, closing up the deck. You're still holding a break with your left little finger above the two black aces. Double-cut the deck at this point, bringing the black aces to the top. (See *Double-Cut,* p. 13.)

As you do the double-cut, say, "Let's mix them up a little. That way, we can all get thoroughly confused."

"Now, for a really difficult feat. Let's see if we can find those reversed red aces." With your right hand, cut off about a third of the deck and turn the packet face up on top. "Let's see if they're here." Even up the deck and then fan through to the first face-down card, letting spectators see that the aces aren't there. (Make sure that you don't fan so fast that you reveal the face-up cards.)

"No luck."

Take off these face-up cards with your right hand. Turn them face down and set them onto the table.

Give the cards a legitimate double-cut, like this: Hold the cards from above in your right hand; with your left hand, take a third of the cards from the bottom and place them on top. Then take another third from the bottom and place them on top.

Turn about a third of the cards face up on top of the deck, saying, "Maybe the reversed red aces are here." Fan through to the first face-down card, just as you did before.

"Nope, not here either."

Lift off the face-up cards, turn them face down, and set them on top of the other pile on the table.

"This is getting tiresome." Fan through the remaining cards until you come to the face-up black aces. "Good heavens! The black aces are face up!" With your right hand, take them from the deck and set them face up on the table. Fan through the rest of the cards, showing that there are no more face-up cards.

"So, what happened to the red aces?" Turn over the packet, fan through to the red aces, take them out, and set them on the table with the black aces.

Now you're ready to perform another ace trick.

Mental

As stated earlier, any force can be used as an exercise in mind reading. Simply force a card and then reveal it bit by bit. You ask the spectator to think of the color, which you name. Next he thinks of the suit; name it. Then he thinks of the value; concentrate fiercely and eventually name the value. Some forces are especially suited to mental work. Here are four.

Top or Bottom Force

Seeking a force that was suitable for telepathy *and* easy, I came up with this one.

You must know and remember the top and bottom cards. Here's a good way to accomplish this: Fan through the deck, saying, "I hope we don't have a joker in here." Note the top and bottom cards. Give the deck two overhand shuffles.

Shuffle one: With the first move you squeeze a bit with your left fingers and left thumb, retaining the top and bottom cards in your left hand. Then shuffle off the rest. This retains the bottom card and brings the top card to second from the bottom.

Shuffle two: Again retain the top and bottom cards with the first move. Shuffle off the rest until you have only a few cards left. Shuffle these on top one by one. The top and bottom cards are now in the same position as when you started.

Deal cards one at a time into a pile on the table, telling a spectator to tell you when to stop. When he says stop, place the pile in your hands next to the one on the table. You know the bottom card of both piles. Say to the spectator, "Please pick up either pile and look at the bottom card."

Either/Or Force

You must know the top card. Deal cards into a pile, telling a spectator to tell you when to stop. As soon as he says stop, start dealing another pile to the right of the first one. Again, the spectator tells you when to stop. Immediately, start dealing a third pile to the *left* of the first one. Once more the spectator tells you when to stop. Place the remaining cards in your hand to the far right.

Four piles are in a row on the table. You know the bottom card of the second pile from your left. Cover the two piles on the right with your outstretched right hand and the two piles on the left with your outstretched left hand. Ask, "Right or left?" Whichever is chosen, push aside the two piles on your right.

"Pick up a pile, please." If he picks up the pile containing the force card, push aside the remaining pile and tell him to look at the bottom card. If he picks up the other pile, take it from him and place it aside with the other discarded piles. Tell him, "Please look at the bottom card of your chosen pile."

This business is called the *equivoque* or the *magician's choice,* of which there are many versions. Try it out; it's quite easy and totally convincing.

Everything's in Order

Here's a more sophisticated version of the previous force. It's a Harry Lorayne version of an old trick.

Pattering about how difficult it is to exert mental control over another person, fan through the cards, faces towards yourself. Decide on one of the top twelve cards and note its position from the top. Let's say you decide on the king of hearts, which is fifth from the top. Fan through the deck again until you come to its mate, the king of diamonds. Place the king of diamonds face down on the table, announcing that this is your prediction.

Then deal out six cards in a face-down row and, below this row (nearer to you), another face-down six-card row. The fifth card from the left in the top row is your force card. (Actually, it could be any one of the cards, so long as you know its position.)

Marcy will assist you. Say, "Marcy, I'd like you to make your decisions as fast as you possibly can. We *must* have your immediate reactions. Ready? Top or bottom row?"

Whatever Marcy replies, you say, "Okay," and immediately gather up the row that does *not* contain the force card. In this instance, you take away the row nearest you and set these cards aside.

Immediately place your right hand on the three cards on the right and your left hand on the three cards on the left. Separate the two groups, asking Marcy, "Left or right?"

Whatever she replies, push aside the group not containing the force card. In this instance, you push aside the three cards on the left.

"Pick up two of the cards," you say. If she leaves the force card on the table, take the two cards from her. Place the remaining card next to your prediction card.

If one of the two she picks up is the force card, push aside the card remaining on the table, saying, "Hand me one of the cards."

If she hands you the force card, place it face down next to your prediction card. If she hands you the other card, toss it aside, take the other card from her, and place it face down next to your prediction card.

"Let's see if you matched my prediction," you say. Turn over both cards together.

As you've noticed, this procedure is an *equivoque,* similar to that described in *Either/Or Force* (p. 74).

Easy Bottom Force

Sneak a peek at the bottom card. Hold the deck in the dealing position in your left hand.

"Some people think a mentalist can tell what a card is by looking at the back. Let's make sure I can't see the back of the card you think of."

While saying this, grip the deck from above with your palm-down right hand, fingers at the front, thumb at the rear. Push all the cards forward on your left hand except the bottom card. The cards should be pushed forward a bit less than an inch. Bevel the cards back towards your body, completely hiding the force card (Illus. 44).

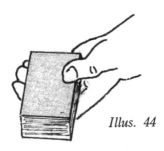

Illus. 44

Ask a spectator to remove a pile of cards *from the bottom of the deck.* After he does so, push the bevelled cards back with your left first finger. Avert your head and, with your right hand, lift up the cards and show the spectator the card at the bottom of your packet. Naturally, it's the force card.

Corresponding Cards

Floyd Shotts invented this trick.

After shuffling the cards, turn them with the faces towards yourself. Say, "I have to find a suitable prediction card. This is very difficult." Puzzle over the cards as you fan through the deck.

Actually you note the bottom card. Counting it as one, you count through the face-up cards until you get to 13. Cut that 13th card to the top. Thus, the card you noted becomes the 13th card from the top of the deck. Continue fanning through the deck until you come to the mate of that original bottom card—the card that matches it in color and value. When you find it, remove it from the deck and place it on the table, saying, "There it is—my prediction card."

Suppose that the mate to the bottom card is among the 13 you're counting from the bottom. No problem. Simply start counting to 13 from *the mate*. As before, cut when you get to 13. In this instance, the mate to the original bottom card will now be 13th from the top. Fan through until you get to the *original bottom card*. Place this face down on the table as your prediction card. It is, of course, the mate to the 13th card from the top.

Set the deck down.

Evelyn will help out. Say, "Evelyn, I'd like you to think of any small number, say 1 to 10. Now you'll have to remember that number. Then, while my back is turned, deal off that many from the top of the deck and hide them." Turn away from the group.

When she finishes, turn back. Take the deck, saying, "Now I'm going to take 12 cards." Count 12 cards into a pile on the table. Pick up the pile and place it behind your back. (If sitting at a table, you can take the cards under the table.)

"Evelyn, I'll bring out the cards one by one. When I bring out the card at your number, tell me to stop."

Behind your back, take off the top card, bring it to the

front and set it face down on the table. Continue with the next top card. Keep on going until Evelyn tells you to stop.

Bring forth the rest of the cards from behind your back and set them aside. The card at which Evelyn stopped you goes face down next to the prediction card.

"If I've correctly predicted the future, these two cards should match."

Turn over the two, showing that they're mates.

Go Figure

Anyone's deck may be used. Say, "I'm now going to construct five poker hands. Once I've finished, I'll never look at the faces of these cards again." Fan through and take out these five values in any order: A 3 5 7 9. The suits should be clubs and diamonds, and you should have three of one suit and two of the other. These cards are tossed out face up in a pile. Pick up the pile and place it face down to your left.

You'll form three more piles in the same way. In these, the suits won't matter.

Fan through and form another face-up pile of these cards: 2 3 6 7 10. This pile is turned face down and set to the right of the first pile.

Again go through the cards, making a face-up pile of these cards: 4 5 6 7 Q. Turn the pile face down and set it to the right of the other two.

The last pile you form consists of 8 9 10 J Q. This pile is turned face down and placed to the right of the other three.

Shuffle the fourth pile and place it face down on the table. Shuffle the third pile and place it on top of it. Shuffle the second pile and place it on the main pile. Shuffle the first pile and place it on top of all.

Say to Bruce, "I'd like you to think of any card at all. So you'll know that there's nothing psychological about this experiment, I'd like you to change your mind and think of another card. Got one? Good."

Now take the top five cards, fan them out, and display them so that only the spectators can see the faces. Ask Bruce if his card is among these. Whatever his answer, these are placed on the bottom of the stack. You now show the next five, ask the same question, and place these on the bottom. Perform the same procedure twice more. At this point, you know the value of Bruce's card.

How? Time for an explanation.

Here are the four groups of cards:

> **1:** A 3 5 7 9
> **2:** 2 3 6 7 10
> **4:** 4 5 6 7 Q
> **8:** 8 9 10 J Q

Note that the first group is numbered **1,** the second group is numbered **2,** the third group is numbered **4,** and the fourth group is numbered **8.** To determine the value of the chosen card, add the numbers of the groups in which the spectator finds his card.

Suppose the spectator finds his card only in groups **1** and **4.** Add these two together and you get 5, the value of his card. Consult the chart and you'll see that the 5 is the only card which appears in both of these groups.

Suppose the spectator sees his card in the first three groups (**1, 2,** and **4).** Add these three numbers and you get 7. Again look at the chart, and note that 7 is the only card that appears in all three groups.

The ace appears only in group **1,** the 2 only in group **2,** and the 4 only in group **4.**

The 8 appears only in group **8,** but the jack appears only in this group also. (Later, I'll explain how these are differentiated.)

The queen has a value of 12 and, therefore, appears in groups **4** and **8.**

If the thought-of card appears in none of the groups, then it's a king.

When you fan out the first five cards, Bruce either sees his card or doesn't. This is the only time that you then ask, "Is your suit here?" If he answers yes, the card is a club or diamond. If he answers no, the card is a heart or spade. You'll use this information later. For this example, assume that Bruce answers yes, so you know that the card is a heart or spade.

Show the other three groups of five, placing each on the bottom. Suppose the card appeared in groups numbered **1** and **8.** The thought-of card, therefore, is a 9.

What about the suit? You must probe. "Think about the suit of your card, please." Concentrate, placing your hands to your temples. "I believe that your card is red." In this example, you've already determined that the card is either a heart or a spade. So if Bruce says yes, you say, "I thought so. Your card is a heart." If he says no, you say, "That's right, that's right. The card is a spade." Concentrate further. "In fact, it's the nine of spades."

If the card is a club or diamond, you follow the same procedure. Announce red, for instance. If you're right, the card is a diamond; if you're wrong, it must be a club.

This trick can and should be repeated.

What if the spectator chooses *only* the fourth group of cards? This group has a value of **8,** and the card could be either an 8 or a jack. You must probe to differentiate the two. My favorite method is this: Concentrating, I say, "I believe that you thought of an even-numbered card." If the spectator immediately answers yes, I know it's an 8, and I say so. But if he hesitates (or, in rare instances, gives a quick negative answer), I know it's the jack. In this instance, I say. "No, no, it's a face card. Let me see. Yes, it's a jack."

Alternatively, you could simply say, "Your card is a face

card." If the answer is yes, the card is the jack. If the answer is no, it's the 8.

Note

There really isn't much memory work in selecting cards for the groups. The first group is odd cards, running from A (one) to 9, and they're clubs or diamonds:

1: A 3 5 7 9

The second group is the only tough one. All you have to remember is that the first two numbers are 2 and 3, two numbers in sequence. Add three to the last number and you get 6. This is followed by 7, the next number in sequence. Add three to the 7, and you get 10.

2: 2 3 6 7 10

The third group is easy. It begins with a 4, of course, and the ensuing numbers follow in sequence. The exception is the last card, a queen.

4: 4 5 6 7 Q

The fourth group is the easiest of all. It begins with an 8, and is completely sequential.

8: 8 9 10 J Q

Sneaky Signal

You can perform astonishing feats of mentalism when you have a confederate. The next three tricks present clever ways in which a confederate can signal a chosen card to you.

You, or your confederate, start by dealing ten cards onto the table, in this formation:

```
    X         X
        X
    X         X
    X         X
        X
    X         X
```

Turn away. Ask a spectator to touch one of the cards. When you turn back, concentrate briefly, and then identify the selected card. This can be repeated a few times.

How *do* you do it? Your partner is holding the remainder of the deck in his left hand. The position of his thumb on the deck signals the position of the card on the table. For example, if the chosen card is the one at the upper left position, your confederate's thumb rests on the upper left corner of the deck. If the spectator chose the card at the upper middle position, your partner's thumb rests on the upper middle portion of the deck. In Illus. 45, the confederate is signalling

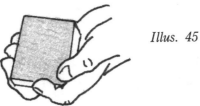

Illus. 45

the card at the upper left. (Obviously, your partner should be sitting or standing so that the deck is in the same relative position as the cards on the table.)

When you attempt to identify the chosen card, do *not* immediately look for the signal. Instead, bend over the table, study the cards, and sneak a quick peek when no one can see your eyes.

After performing the stunt a few times, proceed to the next method.

One Ahead

The cards are laid out as in the previous trick. A spectator touches one of the cards while your back is turned. When you turn back, ask your confederate, "Would you please touch the cards one by one?"

Your partner then touches each of the cards, apparently at random. Actually, by mutual agreement, your confederate touches a card at a particular position just before he touches the chosen card. For instance, he first touches three or four cards. Then he touches the card in the upper middle position—the agreed signal position. The one he touches immediately after that is the chosen card. Before you announce the chosen card, let him finish touching all the cards.

Suppose the spectator has chosen the signal card—in this instance, the one in the upper middle position. Your partner touches some other card first, and then touches another card. He then touches the first card again. You immediately know that the chosen one is the signal card. Let him finish touching the cards, and then name the chosen card.

If you do this version a second time, the agreed signal position should be different from the first one.

Ten Tells

The cards are still laid out in the position described in *Sneaky Signal* (p. 81). As with *One Ahead* (p. 82), when you turn back after a card has been chosen, you ask your assistant to touch the cards one by one.

Your confederate actually *does touch the cards in random order*. Still, you know the name of the selected card. How is this possible?

When the original ten cards were placed on the table, you made sure that *one* ten was among them—let's say, the ten of diamonds. It doesn't matter where the ten of diamonds is placed in the layout.

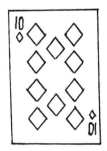

Illus. 46

Take a look at Illus. 46. Notice that the ten is, in fact, a miniature version of the layout on the table, each large diamond standing for one of the cards. When your confederate touches the ten, he simply touches the diamond which matches the position of the chosen card. Suppose the spectator chose the card at the lower left position in the layout. When your confederate gets around to touching the ten of diamonds, he touches it on the diamond in the lower left corner.

This trick can and should be repeated.

Wally Wilson brought this stunt to my attention.

Mind Meld

In the previous three tricks, your assistant was presumably an innocent bystander. In the next two, your assistant is presented as a medium who possesses strong extrasensory powers.

The medium, Mindy, is in the next room, which should be behind you. You're seated in a chair at the table. Spread the deck face up on the table and ask a spectator to touch a card.

Ask someone to call Mindy back. Mindy enters and stands behind you. She says, "I'm about to attempt the famous 'Mind Meld.' She closes her eyes and holds her fingertips to your temples. After considerable concentration, she names the chosen card. The stunt can be repeated.

You, of course, signal the name of the card to her. If you clench your teeth slightly, there will be a slight movement in your temple. A person with fingertips resting lightly on your temples will feel this movement.

You first signal the value of the card by counting out the value with repeated clenches. For a six, for instance, you'd clench six times. (Jacks are 11, queens are 12, and kings are 13.)

After you've signalled the value, pause for three seconds, and then signal the suit. You and your partner need only remember the order of clubs, hearts, spades, diamonds. (CHaSeD is the traditional mnemonic.) Clubs would be one clench, hearts two, spades three, and diamonds four.

Just practise a bit to make sure that you and the "medium" are attuned.

Easy Choice

As with the previous trick, Mindy is the medium. This trick requires some preparation, however. You must set up a deck so that red cards alternate with black cards. Set the deck on the table.

"Mindy, our medium, must leave the room while we have some cards chosen."

After Mindy leaves, have several spectators give the deck a complete cut. Have Darren give the deck a complete cut and then take the top card. Ask Herman to take the next top card.

"You must each look at your card and commit it to memory."

This next bit is most important. Have Darren place his card on top of the deck. Then Herman places his card on top. Thus, the cards have been replaced in reverse order.

Again, have the deck given several complete cuts. Pick up the deck, saying, "Since two persons have chosen cards, we must have a pile for each person."

Deal the deck into two piles, alternately going from one pile to the other. The deck is now divided into two halves. Each half contains all of the same color with the exception of one of the chosen cards.

"Darren and Herman, I'd like each of you to pick up one pile and take it to Mindy." When the two approach Mindy, she holds out her hands, taking one pile in each hand. She sets one pile down. Fanning through the other pile, she seems to concentrating fiercely. (Naturally, she doesn't let Darren and Herman see the faces of the cards.) Actually, she's looking for the only card in the group of the opposite color. Mindy removes this card and places it face down in front of her.

She picks up the other pile, *adding it to those she's holding.* She fans through the added cards and finds the only one of the opposite color. This, too, she places face down in front of her. Mindy casually shuffles the deck as she says something like, "I felt certain vibrations as I looked through the cards, leading me to make my choices. But the vibrations weren't strong, so I could easily be mistaken."

She sets the deck aside and picks up the two cards. As each man names his card, she turns the appropriate one over and presents it to him.

Notice that the deck has been mixed so that there's no clue as to how the trick was performed.

Gambling

Impossible Poker Deal

"I'd like to demonstrate a poker deal," you say, fanning through the cards. "I'll need lower-value cards. Gamblers don't want aces and face cards when they make their big killings. Those cards are so obvious that people might suspect the gamblers of cheating."

Remove all the cards from 2 to 7, tossing them face up on the table. Set the rest of the deck aside. Pick up the low cards and fan them out, faces towards yourself, saying, "Let's get some pairs here."

The statement is a form of misdirection. Actually, you'll remove three 3s, three 5s, and three 7s—three trios of *odd* cards, but you'll collect these cards in pairs. First toss out two face-down 3s. On top of them, toss a 3 and a 5. On top of the pile, toss two 5s. Finally, place *three* 7s on top of all.

Turn to Hal and ask, "Would you please shuffle these while

I get some more pairs?" Hal shuffles the nine odd cards while you proceed.

Now gather three trios of *even* cards, using the same misdirection. Toss out two face-down 2s, a 2 and a 4, two 4s, and three 6s. Put the rest of the cards back on the deck.

Have Hal set his cards aside and shuffle the packet you just collected. When he's finished shuffling, say, "Hal, you can place either packet on top of the other." After he puts the packets together, proceed by having Hal deal two hands.

I prefer, however, to give the spectators some reason to feel that, in some way, I'm exerting control. I hold out my left hand and ask the spectator to place the packet in my hand. I place my right hand flat on top of the packet and give my hands a quick up-and-down movement. "A little shake does the job," I say. In fact, I do this "little shake" before each deal.

Let's assume that you've done the "little shake." Hand the cards back to Hal and ask him to deal two five-card poker hands face down, one to you and one to himself. Hal does so, alternately dealing a card to you and a card to himself.

When he finishes, say, "Remember, you shuffled the cards yourself." Turn over the two hands, showing that you have the winner.

The two hands are on the table face up. Place your cards face up on top of his. Turn the combined hands face down. Take the undealt cards and place them face down on top of the combined packet, saying, "You might as well deal the rest of the cards into two hands."

Perform the "little shake," and have him deal again.

Once more you win. Put your face-up cards on top of his, as before. Turn the combined hands face down. This time the combined hands go *on top* of the undealt cards.

Pick up the packet and give it a "little shake." Say to Hal, "The problem is, you don't get to make any choices. The cards are dealt, and you have to accept what you get." Deal a face-up card to him and one to yourself. "But now you'll have the advantage of choosing your cards. You can decide if you want each card. If you don't want it, I get it."

Turn over the next card on the packet. "Do you want this card?" If he wants it, deal it to him face up. If he declines the card, add it, face up, to your hand. Continue until each of you has five cards. (Once Hal has five cards, you get enough more to complete your hand.)

Again, you're a winner.

Place your face-up cards on top of his, asking, "Now do you want to deal, or do you want me to deal?" If *you* are to deal, place the combined pile on top of the undealt packet and deal. If *he* is to deal, place the undealt packet on top of the combined pile, and hand him the cards. In either instance, don't forget that vital "little shake."

Naturally, you win again.

Note

How does the trick work? In an older trick, only ten cards were used: three sets of three-of-a-kind with one separate card. The separate card is always referred to as the "Jonah" card—with good reason. When the ten cards are dealt out, the person with the Jonah card cannot win. (Try it out.)

This trick is subtly set up so that the same system operates. In each deal, *you* get either all odd cards or all even cards. The *spectator* gets only *four* odd cards or *four* even cards. If he gets four odd cards, he always receives one even card, the Jonah. If he gets four even cards, he always receives one odd card, the Jonah. He *cannot* win.

Set 'em Up!

First, secretly get the aces to the top of the deck. If you used the aces a few tricks before, you can simply locate them and cut them to the top. You say, "It's easy to stack the cards when the deck's face down, but people might see too much when you try it face up. Well, I'll stack a great hand to come to me in a four-handed game, and watch for any significant cards as I shuffle."

Hold the deck in the overhand-shuffle position, only with the *face* of the deck against your left thumb. Turn so that your left side is towards the spectators, so that they can see the faces as you shuffle.

Now perform four shuffles. In each shuffle, begin by drawing off the top and bottom cards together. In the first shuffle, you draw these off, and then draw off eleven cards singly with your left thumb. The remaining cards are not thrown on top, but below the others in your left hand.

Second shuffle: Draw off top and bottom together. Draw off eight cards singly, and then drop the rest below those you've shuffled.

Third shuffle: Draw off top and bottom together and then run five cards singly, dropping the rest behind.

Fourth shuffle: Draw off top and bottom together, run two cards singly, and drop the rest below.

When you finish the stack, keep the cards face up and deal out four hands, asking, "You didn't see any aces, did you?"

The effect is quite dramatic as the aces show up in your hand one by one.

Summary of the stack: After drawing off top and bottom together, the numbers you run off singly are 11, 8, 5, and 2. Start with 11 and subtract 3 each time.

Double-Surprise Poker Demo

Fan through the deck, faces towards yourself, putting the aces and kings on top in no special order. While doing this, mention that you'd like to demonstrate how gamblers cheat unsuspecting victims, and that you'll use the four kings to make your point. Pick out the four kings, tossing them out face up. Make sure that spectators don't see the aces, which are now on top.

"In the old riverboat days, people were pretty unsophisticated. Typically, a gambler would get the cards he wanted on the bottom of the deck—in this case, the kings." Place the kings on the bottom of the deck. "Then the gambler would make sure they stayed there."

Give the deck a few riffle shuffles, keeping the kings on the bottom and (just as important) the aces on top.

"Then the gambler would deal out the poker hands. The first round would always be straight, to throw off suspicious players."

While saying this, deal five cards, the beginning of five poker hands. The fifth card goes to you.

"Now come the bottom deals."

On the next four hands, deal the first four cards regularly, but deal the fifth card (the one that goes to your hand) from the bottom. You don't have to do it fast or well; after all, you're demonstrating how poorly it used to be done.

When you're done dealing, gather up the four other hands *one on top of the other,* and place them on top of the deck. Show that you have indeed dealt yourself the four kings and place your hand on top.

"That's the way they used to do it. Now gamblers are much more sophisticated. They stack the cards. Watch."

Perform a false overhand shuffle. (See *Controlling a Group of Cards,* p. 22.) Make sure you take less than half the deck as you begin the shuffle so that you will preserve the top 25 cards in order. Perform a second false overhand shuffle. You might even throw in a false cut.

Deal five hands, saying, "Notice that with stacking, the deal is perfectly legitimate. No bottom deals, no sleight of hand." Continue with similar patter as you complete the deal.

Gather up the other four hands one on top of the other, and place them on top of the deck. Square up your cards. Turn them over on the table, showing just the top indifferent card.

"I, of course, end up with the four kings." Move the top card aside, revealing an ace. "Whoops!" Pause for a moment, giving the spectators a chance to react. Then spread out the rest of the hand. "Well, four aces. That's almost as good."

Put the ace hand on the bottom of the deck. Say, "You're probably wondering what happened to the four kings. I'll show you."

False-shuffle and false-cut as before, and deal. This time, however, when you come to your hand, deal each card face up. It makes for an arresting climax as the spectators see the kings arrive one by one.

Incidentally, after you get all four kings, stop the deal—the trick is over.

Preparation

Two-Faced Card Trick—1

For the next two startling tricks, you'll need a double-faced card. Such cards can be purchased at your local magic shop. But for our purposes, you can just as easily make up your own. Simply take two cards and glue them back to back, making sure they're precisely even.

This first trick was reported by Harry Riser in *MUM,* the publication of the Society of American Magicians.

Let's say that your double-backed card has the jack of spades (JS) on one side and the ten of hearts (10H) on the other. You'll also need a regular JS and 10H. Have the double-faced card in your pocket, with the 10H side facing out.

To start, take the legitimate JS and 10H from your pocket and show both sides of both. "I'd like to try an experiment with these two cards—the JS and the 10H." Place the two cards back to back and square them up. Still keeping them squared, turn over the two, displaying first one side and then the other.

Ask Sean to assist you. Place the two cards into his pocket, with the 10H facing out.

"Sean, where's the 10H?" Naturally, he replies that it's in his pocket. "And the JS is in the same pocket, right?" Of course. "So if I take the 10H from your pocket, like this . . ." Remove the 10H from his pocket. ". . . then you would still have the JS in your pocket. And now *I'll* have the 10H in *my* pocket." Suiting action to words, place the 10H *face out* into your pocket, *behind the double card.*

With a laugh, say, "I think we all understand now that the JS is in your pocket and the 10H is in mine. But let's check to make absolutely sure." Remove the JS from Sean's pocket and hand it to him. Remove the double-faced card from your pocket, displaying the 10H side. (Make sure no one sees the other side of the card.)

Holding the 10H in the dealing position in your left hand, take the JS from Sean with your right hand. Turn it face down and place it under the double-faced card. Apparently the JS and the 10H are now back to back. Even up the cards and display both sides. Put both cards into Sean's pocket, with the legitimate JS facing out. Behind it, of course, is the double card with the 10H side facing his body.

Now comes a very sneaky piece of business based on an ambiguity in the expression "Pick a card for me." It can mean either "Do me a favor and pick a card," or "The card you name will become my card." So say to Sean, "Pick a card for me, Sean—10H or JS." If he chooses the JS, say, "Okay, you picked the JS for me." If he chooses the 10H, say, "You picked the 10H, so I get the JS."

Reach into Sean's pocket and remove the double-faced card, showing the JS. (Practise this move. Needless to say, it's vital that no one see the other side of the card.) Place the double card into your pocket behind the legitimate 10H.

Pause a moment, staring into space. Shake your head. "I keep forgetting. What card do you have?" He says that he has the 10H. Ask him to remove the card from his pocket. It's the JS. You remove the legitimate 10H from your pocket.

Casually show both sides of the two cards and put them away.

Two-Faced Card Trick—2

Let's try another stunt with a double-faced card. Reported by Martin Gardner, this was a specialty of Bert Allerton's.

Again, assume that the double-faced card has the JS on one side and the 10H on the other. You'll also need a regular JS and 10H. Place the JS face up on the table. On top of it, place the 10H face up. On top of all, place the double-faced card, with the JS side up.

Place all three in your pocket with the two-faced card on the outside, JS side facing out.

Start by removing the two outermost cards from your pocket, making sure that spectators don't see the other side of the double-faced card. Fan the two out, showing the JS on top and the 10H below it (Illus. 47). The JS, of course, is the

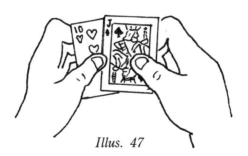

Illus. 47

double-faced card. "As you notice, we have the JS and the 10H." Close up the two cards and turn them over, showing the back. Ask, "Can you remember what the two cards are?" Turn the two face up once more. "That's right, the JS and the 10H." Move the JS below the 10H. Move it back on top again. Close up the two cards and turn them over, showing the back. "What are they again?" Turn them face up and fan them. "That's right."

Ostensibly, you've shown the backs and fronts of both cards.

Place the double-faced card on the table; naturally the JS side is up. Now perform an easy sleight known as *Wild Card Turnover*. With your right hand, hold the 10H at the lower right corner with your thumb on top and fingers beneath. Place your left first finger on the lower left corner of the card on the table. (See Illus. 33, p. 49.) Slide the card in your right hand beneath the right side of the card on the table and, with a counterclockwise move, flip both cards over. Release your grip on the 10H as you complete the move. Logic tells us that both cards should now be face down, but (as you'll discover) logic doesn't prevail. On the table now is a face-up 10H (the other side of the double-faced card) and a face-down 10H. In your pocket is the JS, facing outward.

With your right hand, pick up the face-up 10H (the two-faced card) and place it *behind* the card in your pocket. Make sure no one sees the other side as you place it in the pocket with the 10H side out. In what seems to be an attempt to fool the spectators, as you place the card in your pocket, say, "Now I'll put the JS into my pocket." As you say this, look as shifty-eyed and sneaky as you possibly can.

With your right hand, point to the card on the table. "So what's this card?" The group won't be deceived by your miscalling of the card you placed in your pocket. Someone's bound to say, "*That's* the JS."

"No, no," you say, pulling the outermost card from your pocket and tossing it onto the table. "*This* is the JS. The other card is the 10H." Turn it over. Pick up the JS, casually show its back and drop it face up onto the 10H. Pick up the two and place them, faces outward, in the pocket *behind* the double-faced card. (You'll recall that the double-faced card has its 10H side facing out.)

Apparently, you're done. "Did you like that?" Pause. "Maybe you'd like to see it again."

Remove the two outermost cards from your pocket. This time, simply fan them face up without showing the backs. On top is the 10H side of the double-faced card; below it is the face-up JS. Drop the double-faced card on the table, ostensibly the 10H. With the JS, perform *Wild Card Turnover* (p. 94). On the table the spectators see the JS side of the double-faced card and a face-down card. Pick up the double-faced card, saying, "Now I place the 10H in my pocket." Place the card *behind* the 10H in your pocket. Point to the card on the table. "What's the other card?" You'll be told that the other card is actually the 10H. Pull the outermost card from your pocket, saying, "No, no. *This* is the 10H." Turn over the other card. "This one is the JS." As before, casually show the back of the 10H, drop it on top of the JS, and place the two, faces outward, in your pocket behind the double-faced card.

Again, pretend briefly to be done. Then say, "Would you like to see how it's done?" They will. "Actually, I use three cards."

Remove the two outermost cards from your pocket and separate them on the table. Spectators will see a JS and a 10H. Actually, they're seeing the JS side of the double-faced card.

Explain, "I actually use *two* jacks of spades." Pull the jack of spades about halfway out of your pocket so that all can see it. Push it back into your pocket.

Pick up the 10H and turn both tabled cards over, using *Wild Card Turnover*. Spectators now see the 10H side of the double-faced card and a face-down card. Pick up the double-faced card, apparently the 10H, and place it in your pocket behind the other card as you say, "I actually put the

10H in my pocket, but I call it the JS to confuse you." Pause a moment, saying, "It's really quite easy. You see, I just reach into my pocket and take out the *other* JS." Take the outermost card (JS) from your pocket and toss it onto the table.

Someone's bound to say, "But what about the JS that's still on the table?"

Shake your head. "I'm afraid you're really not paying attention. That isn't the jack of spades . . ." Turn the face-down card over. ". . . That's the 10H."

Casually show both sides of both cards and put them away.

Lucky 7

I developed a slight variation of a Lin Searles trick.

There's an easy setup: You have a face-down seven on top, followed by seven face-up cards.

Charlene should be willing to assist. Say to her, "Charlene, I'd like you to choose a card, but let's make sure that you choose one completely by chance. When I give you the deck, I'd like you to place it behind your back." (If you're seated at a table, she should take the deck under the table.) Give her the deck, making sure no one is behind her to see what goes on.

When the deck is behind her back, continue: "Now please cut off a good-sized pile from the top of the deck and turn the pile over so that it's face up on top."

Turn away and continue the directions: "Even up the cards. Now bring the deck forward and fan through the face-up cards to the first face-down card. Set down all the face-up cards for a moment. Next, look at that first face-down card, the one you cut to. This is your chosen card, so you must remember it. After you look, leave it face down on top of the packet. Now pick up that pile you cut off and place it *face down* on top of the deck." Make sure you give all the directions slowly and clearly so that Charlene understands every step.

Turn back and take the pack from Charlene. With your right hand, take off the top card, making sure no one sees its face. Say, "Behind my back, I'll stick this card face up somewhere in the deck." Your left hand takes the deck behind your back, while your right hand takes the card behind your back.

"Let's see. I'll put it in face up right about . . . there." Actually, you simply place the card face down on top of the deck. Bring the deck forward. Turn it face up. Start fanning through the cards.

"With the deck face up, the card I stuck in should now be face down." Fan through to the face-down card. Set aside all the cards you fanned through to arrive at the face-down card.

"Ah, here's my card. Let's see what it is." Turn it face up and drop it on the table. "Perfect! A seven. That's my lucky number. Let's count down seven cards. What was your card?" Charlene names it. You deal off seven cards, and hers shows up as the last card in the count.

Color Confusion

Don Smith created this trick; I adjusted the handling somewhat. You'll need a red-backed deck and a blue-backed deck. Remove seven cards from the blue-backed deck. Make sure there are at least three spot cards on the bottom of the blue-backed deck. Take eight assorted face cards from the red-backed deck. Place one of these in your pocket. The rest go on the bottom of the blue-backed deck.

The situation: You have a blue-backed deck from which seven cards have been removed. At the bottom of this deck are seven red-backed face cards. Directly above these are at least three blue-backed spot cards. In your pocket is a red-backed face card. Place the deck into the blue-card case. (Get rid of all other cards.)

In performance, remove the deck from its card case. Hold the deck face down and casually fan through about two-thirds of the cards, saying, "Let's try an experiment with these cards." Make sure you don't get to the red-backed cards. Don't call attention to the color of the backs. The fanning should be sufficient to establish this.

Close up the deck. Turn it over. "On the bottom, I have a group of face cards." Fan through them, showing them, and fan a few cards past them. As you close up the fan of face cards with your palm-up right hand, add a spot card at the back. Lift the packet off with your right hand as you set aside the balance of the deck face down. Even up the packet.

You're about to perform the *flustration count,* a sneaky maneuver attributed to Brother John Hamman. It isn't a difficult sleight. In fact, it's not a sleight at all, but an easy, subtle move which is totally deceptive. In performing the *flustration count,* you'll casually demonstrate that all the cards in the packet you're holding have blue backs, even though only one of the cards actually does have a blue back.

Now you're holding the packet from above in your right hand, fingers at the outer end and thumb at the inner end. (If you have shorter fingers, your right first finger may be resting on top near the outer end.) Turn your right hand palm up, displaying the blue back of the top card. Turn your right hand palm down. With your left thumb, draw off the card on the face of the deck (Illus. 48). Hold this card in your left hand. Draw off another card from the face of the deck with your left

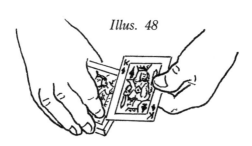

Illus. 48

thumb, letting the card land face up on top of the other card in your left hand. Casually turn over your right hand, showing the back of the top card again. Draw off two more cards individually. Once more show the back of the top card. Turn your right hand palm down and place the packet in your right hand face up on the table. Take the face-up cards from your left hand into your right hand and place these face up on top of those on the table. Pick up the packet with your right hand and place it face down in your left hand.

"Let's add a card." With your right hand, remove the red-backed face card from your pocket, showing only the back. "This one should be easy to tell from the others." Insert the card face down into the middle of the packet. Turn the packet face up and cut it several times.

Fan out the cards so that all can see the faces. Ask, "So what was the card we added?"

Spectators notice the spot card and name it.

"And do you remember the color of its back?"

The answer is "Red."

"Oh, how quickly we forget," you say. Take the spot card out and turn it over. It has a blue back. Pause a moment. "And you probably forgot that all these are red." Turn the packet over and spread it out, showing the red backs.

Miscellaneous

Let Us Gather Together

This trick is by Stewart James; I made a simple adjustment.

Anna will probably be delighted to shuffle the deck for you. Take the cards back. Hold the cards so that both you and the spectators can see the faces as you fan them from hand to hand. Say, "I'll have to find three cards of the same value." Fan all the way through so that you can note the value of the fourth card from the top. (If one of the top three is of the same value, have the deck shuffled again.)

Suppose that the fourth card from the top is the six of spades. Close up the cards and start fanning from the bottom again. You're looking for the other three sixes. As you come to each one, toss it face up onto the table. "Let's find three sixes. My guess is that two of them will be of the same color, and one of them will be of a different color."

Hold the deck in your left hand. With your right hand, place the sixes in a row. The two cards on your right should be of the same color (in the example, the six of hearts and the six of diamonds). The one on your left is the odd-colored card (the six of clubs).

"The six of clubs is the different-colored one, so that's the one I'll try to control." Turn the three cards face down. "So let's see if I can control the six of clubs."

Fan off three cards from the top of the deck. Place them on the card on the left. Pick up all four cards and place them on top of the deck. As you close up the four cards on top, get a small break with your left little finger under the top one. Immediately transfer the break to your right thumb. Perform a double-cut, bringing the top card to the bottom of the deck. (See *Double-Cut,* p. 13.)

Again fan off three cards from the top of the deck. Place them on one of the other sixes. Pick up the four cards and place them on top. Proceed exactly as before, cutting the top card to the bottom.

Perform the same procedure with the last card on the table.

"Now I've been trying to keep track of the six of clubs. Let's see how I did." Turn over the top card and place it on the table. "There it is."

Pause for a moment. "Oh, yes . . ." Deal the next two cards face up on the table. "Here are the other two sixes."

Again, pause. "Oh, what the heck!" Turn over the next card, the six of spades, and deal it face up on the table.

Pop-Up Card

While chatting with the spectators, hold the deck in the dealing position in your left hand. Grip the deck from above with your right hand, fingers at the front, thumb at the rear. With your right thumb, riffle the top few cards slightly, separating the top two cards from the rest of the deck. Hold a break below these two with the tip of your left little finger.

Even up the cards at the ends with your right hand. Now simply *lift off* the top two cards with your second and third fingers at the front and your thumb at the rear. Hold the double card straight up so all can see it; then bend it almost in half so that the top of the face of the double card almost meets the bottom. Replace the double card on the deck, holding the center down with your left thumb. Take the top card in your right hand, thumb on top and fingers below. Hold this card sideways so all can see that it's bent downwards at the ends. Slide the card into the middle of the deck. Incidentally, as you take off this card, make sure your left thumb continues its pressure, holding down the center of the next card.

Grip the deck from above with your right hand, curling your first finger under so that it, rather than your left thumb, is now holding down the top card at the center. Move up the deck in your left hand, holding it at the sides between thumb and fingertips. Squeeze at the sides to prevent the top card from popping up. Take your right hand away and hold the deck up sideways so that all can see.

Say, "One, two, three." On "three," release the pressure of the fingers and thumb on the sides, and the card will visibly pop up at the middle about a quarter-inch or so. As I say, "Three," I usually snap the fingers of my right hand to add emphasis. With your right hand, carefully lift off the card, showing that it's risen from the middle of the deck.

Don't repeat the trick.

Those Mysterious Ladies

A card is chosen and replaced in the deck. Four queens are dealt out face down. The spectator chooses one, and it mysteriously changes to his chosen card.

"I'm going to need four mysterious cards," you say. Fan through the deck and remove the four queens, placing them face down in a pile on the table. Do this without showing their faces. First remove a red queen, then another red queen, followed by the black queens. So, from the bottom up, the pile on the table consists of two red queens and two black queens.

Have Evan select a card as you say, "You need to choose a card to represent you." The card is taken, shown around, and replaced in the deck. You cleverly bring it to the top. The way I cleverly do it is with a double-cut (see *Double-Cut,* p. 13), but you may use any other method. (See *Controlling a Card,* p. 13.)

Turn the deck face up and fan the cards from the bottom somewhat (not revealing the top card, of course), saying, "You could have chosen any of these cards to represent you." Close up the fan. "Now it's time to examine the mysterious cards." Place the deck face up on the queen pile. Pick up all the cards with your right hand, turning them over and placing them in your left hand.

"Four mysterious cards," you say. "And what could be more mysterious than four lovely ladies?"

Fan out the four face-up queens with your right hand, pushing off an additional card below them. As you push the queens back, obtain a little-finger break beneath the fifth card. With your right hand, from above, take the cards with your thumb at the near end and fingers at the outer end.

Draw off the top queen onto the deck with your left thumb. Using the left edge of the remaining cards in your right hand, flip it face down. "Here we have a lovely redhead," you say. Turn the next queen the same way, saying, "And another gorgeous redhead." Flip it face down as before. Turn over the next queen, saying, "A mighty pretty brunette." As you flip this queen face down, drop the two cards remaining in your right hand (presumably one card) on top of the deck. "And yet another attractive brunette." Push this last queen to the left with your left thumb and then, with your right fingers, flip it face down.

From the top down, the top four cards are black queen, chosen card, black queen, red queen. (The other red queen, irrelevant to the rest of the trick, is the fifth card down.) Spread out the top four cards and take them from the deck in your right hand. Set the rest of the deck aside.

Say to Evan, "Now you're going to have to choose one of these beautiful young ladies."

You're about to perform an easy maneuver known as *The Olram Subtlety.* Place the packet of four cards into your left hand so that they're considerably forward of the regular dealing position (Illus. 49). (This is so that when you turn your

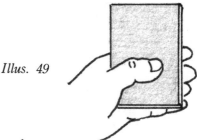

Illus. 49

left hand palm down, the bottom card can be easily seen.) Draw the top card off the front end of the face-down packet with your right hand. The instant it clears, turn both hands over. Your right hand displays the card just drawn off (a black queen), and your left hand displays the bottom card of the three-card packet (a red queen) (Illus. 50). Turn both hands palm down, immediately dropping the card from your right hand face down and—*at the same time*—thumbing off the top card of those in your left hand, letting it land to the left of the card that comes from your right hand.

Illus. 50

With your right hand, draw off the top card of the two remaining cards. Again, turn both hands over, displaying the faces. Turn your hands palm down. Simultaneously drop the card in your right hand to the right of the two on the table while dropping the card in your left hand to the left of those on the table.

Apparently, you've shown all four queens. Actually, you've shown a red queen twice. From your left to right, the cards on the table are red queen, chosen card, black queen, black queen. Let's assume that the chosen card is the seven of clubs. The layout could be this, as you look at it:

QH   7C   QC   QS

You now do an *equivoque* or *magician's choice* similar to that described in *Either/Or Force* (p. 74). Say to Evan, "Pass your hands over those cards, and when you feel ready, let each hand fall onto a card." He covers two of the cards with his hands. If one of the two is the chosen card, pull the other two cards towards you, saying, "Now please hand me one of those." If he hands you the chosen card, say, "So this is your free choice." Set the card face down directly in front of him. If he hands you the other card, drop it down with the others which you pulled out of line. Point to the card under his card, saying, "Your choice."

Suppose he covers two cards other than the chosen card. Indicate that he is to lift his hands. You pull the two cards towards you. As before, ask him to hand you one of the remaining two.

In all instances, Evan gets his chosen card. Turn the queens face up one by one, saying, "Here we have the poor ladies who weren't chosen." Toss them face down onto the deck.

"So you've chosen a red-haired lady. The question is, would she choose you? What was the name of the card representing you?" Evan names it, and you have him turn it over. "Excellent. You *were* chosen, and everyone lives happily ever after."

If performing the trick for a woman, use the four kings. In the patter, they become two redheaded men and two dark-haired men. When you pick up the kings so that they are face up on the face-down deck, fan them out, as with the queens. The patter changes slightly, however. "We have four mysterious men."

Good Choice

Here's a fast, clever trick requiring only nerve and a bit of practice.

In your pocket, you have four kings. The king of spades and the king of clubs have blue backs. The king of hearts and the king of diamonds have red backs. The order doesn't matter.

Remove the four cards from your pocket, making sure spectators cannot see any of the backs. Hold them face up in your left hand. Spread the kings out and ask Ted to name one (Illus. 51). After he does so, say, "You can change your mind if you want to, Ted—it doesn't matter." When he finally decides on one, remove it from the group, saying, "This one." Replace it so that it's the lowermost of the face-up cards. Maneuver the other cards about so that the king that's of the same color as the one chosen is at the face of the packet. As you do this, say, "You could have chosen this one, or this one, whatever one you wished." Tell him that he can still change his mind. If he does, maneuver the cards so that they're in the appropriate position described.

Illus. 51

You are about to perform a variation of the *flustration count*, previously described in the trick *Color Confusion*, p. 97.

Close up the face-up packet and hold it from above in your right hand, fingers at the outer end and thumb at the inner end. Turn your right hand palm up, displaying the back of the top, chosen, card. Let's assume he has selected the king of clubs. Say, "It's amazing that you should choose the king of clubs, which has a *blue* back." Turn your right hand palm down. With the left *fingers*, draw the king of clubs from the back of the packet into your left hand. (This first maneuver differs from the standard *flustration count*.) Turn your right hand palm up again, displaying a red-backed card. Turn your hand palm down and, with your left thumb, draw off the card at the *face* of the packet so that it comes to rest on top of the king of clubs. (This is the standard move in the *flustration count*.) Perform the action again. Then display the back of the last card, turn your right hand palm down and drop the card face up on top of those in your left hand.

Ted has chosen the only card with a different-colored back.

Note

If you wish, repeat the trick several times. Simply put the cards into your pocket. Chat for a moment about what a coincidence has occurred. Then say, "I have another set of kings in my pocket." Dig into a different pocket. "No luck. Maybe they're here." Take the same set of kings from your pocket and repeat the trick. You might even put the kings away again and then go through the same routine. The basic trick is so deceptive that there's little danger that spectators will catch on, and it becomes quite amusing when spectators suspect that you're using the same kings.

Spin-Out!

Reinhard Muller created this quick, simple, startling effect.

Remove from the deck the two red aces, setting them aside face down without showing them. Have a card chosen and bring it to the bottom of the deck. The easiest way is to secure a little-finger break below the chosen card and then do a double-cut. (See *Double-Cut,* p. 13.)

Hold the deck from above in your left hand, fingers on one side, thumb on the other side. Pick up one of the aces, show it, and place it face up on the bottom. As you reach out with your right hand to pick up the other ace, draw back the ace on the bottom slightly with your left fingers (Illus. 52).

Illus. 52   *Bottom view*

Place the second ace face up on top of the deck. Still retaining the left-hand grip, grasp the front of the deck with your right hand. Your right thumb is on top, your right first finger on the selection, and your right second finger on a red ace (Illus. 53).

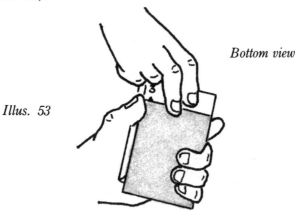

Bottom view

Illus. 53

The following move sounds a bit difficult; in fact, you'll master it after a few tries. Let loose of the left-hand grip. Simultaneously, with the right hand revolve the deck forward, and, in a snappy dealing motion, toss the cards onto the table, but not *all* the cards. You cling to the three cards you're gripping with your right thumb and first and second fingers—the two aces and the selected card.

Fan the three cards with your right hand (Illus. 54). Turn the fan over, showing that "the selected card, hidden in the middle of the deck, has been captured by the aces!"

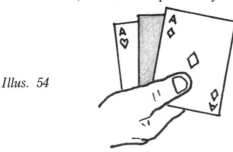

Illus. 54

Two-Time Turnabout

Charles Jordan invented this wonderful trick; after considerable experimentation, I decided to combine the Jordan trick with a clever principle from another old trick.

All you require is a deck of cards, a rubber band, and a handkerchief.

Ask Vicki to assist you. Hand her the deck and ask her to shuffle the cards. Say, "I'm going to turn my back and I'd like you to take out any one of the cards, look at it, and hand it around so everyone can see what it is."

Turn your back. After she's taken out her card, hold your hands behind your back and say, "Please give me the rest of the deck." After she does so, turn and face the group. Take off the top card of the deck, turn the rest of the deck face up, and drop the card on top. This should be done quite rapidly. Immediately bring the deck forward. The cards are all face up except for the top card, which is face down.

While doing this, chat along these lines: "You've freely selected a card. Once it's returned to the deck, we're going to make sure it cannot possibly escape." By this time, you should be facing the group.

Pick up the rubber band and place it around the middle of the deck. Keep the deck tilted forward slightly so that no one can see that the bottom card is actually face up. Take back the chosen card and slide it face down into the middle of the pack.

"The magical rubber band will guard your card," you explain. "Now let's try the magical handkerchief on the magical deck of cards." With your right hand, whip out a handkerchief and spread it over your left hand and the cards. Just as the handkerchief descends, put your left thumb under the deck and flip the deck over. Snap your right-hand fingers, and whip off the handkerchief, tossing it aside.

Remove the rubber band from the deck and begin fanning

through the cards as you ask, "And what was the name of your card?"

Vicki names her card. You continue fanning through the pack and stop when you come to her face-up card. "Despite the rubber-band," you declare, "your card has turned over in the deck!"

Casually continue fanning through the face-down cards, stopping short of the bottom, of course, so that the face-up card on the bottom won't show up. Fan back through the deck to the chosen card. Separate the cards at this point, taking all the cards *above* the chosen card into your right hand. With your left thumb push off the face-up chosen card and take it at the top of the packet in your right hand. Place the packet in your right hand back on top of the packet in your left hand. Even up the cards. You have simply placed the face-up chosen card on top of the deck.

"So here it is, your chosen card . . ." Name it. ". . . face up on top of the deck. Now let's try another experiment."

The situation is this. The chosen card is face up on top, and another card is face up on the bottom.

"For the magic to work, you must perform some mystic rites with the deck. *And* you must perform these rites behind your back. So, Vicki, please put your hands behind your back." Position her so that no one can see behind her. "Open your left hand, please."

You're holding the deck in the dealing position in your left hand. *With your left hand only,* place the deck behind her back. The minute the deck is out of sight, turn your left hand palm down, reversing the deck. Place the pack in her left hand. Stand close by to keep her from bringing the deck forward until you're ready.

Give the following directions, with appropriate pauses: "Take the top card—your chosen card—turn it face down, and stick it into the middle of the deck. Give the cards a complete cut. Turn the deck over, and give the cards another complete cut. Turn the deck over, and give the cards another cut. Now, just turn the deck over. That completes the mystic ritual. Give me the cards, please." *Three* times Vicki has cut the cards and turned the pack over.

She brings the deck forward and hands it to you. You now perform the same procedure with the rubber band and the handkerchief as you did before, only this time you do nothing tricky. Snap your fingers, whip the handkerchief aside, and remove the rubber band. Fan through the cards, saying, "I wonder what happened to your card this time. Good heavens! It turned over again."

Fan through the entire deck, demonstrating, but not *saying,* that the remainder of the cards are all face down.

Wedded Bliss

This is Werner Miller's clever concoction; I've made the trick more amusing and have changed the ending.

Remove from the deck all the kings and queens as you chat about how important a good marriage is. "Here," for instance, "we have four loving, loyal couples." Without calling attention to the suits, lay the eight cards out like this (your view):

KC QC KH QH
KS QS KD QD

Note that in the top row you have the club marriage, followed by the heart marriage. In the second row you have the spade marriage, followed by the diamond marriage. (In other words, the couples are in CHaSeD order.)

Gesture towards the layout. "Just look at those happy couples!" Turn all the cards face down in place. "No matter how you split them up, they always want to be back together." Exchange the fourth card in the top row with the third card in the second row; exchange the second card in the top row with the first card in the second row. (In other words, exchange the QH and KD, and then the QC and KS.) The layout now (with the cards face down):

$$
\begin{array}{cccc}
\text{KC} & \text{KS} & \text{KH} & \text{KD} \\
\text{QC} & \text{QS} & \text{QH} & \text{QD}
\end{array}
$$

Ask Myrna to assist you. Turn the KH face up, saying, "Here we have a happy king. Myrna, do you think you can find his mate, the QH?" Surprisingly, hardly anyone can pick out the QH on the first try, and very seldom on the second try.

If Myrna should get it on her first attempt, compliment her on how observant she is. If she misses, show the card she chose and turn it face down again. "I'll give you another chance, Myrna." If she gets it, praise her as before. But if not, show the card she chose and turn it face down. "Now Myrna, I wish you'd stop fooling around. Which one is the QH?"

If she misses as many as four times, I usually tap the QH and ask, "Have you tried this one yet?" When she finally gets it, turn the card face up and offer congratulations. Set aside the KH and QH face up, fanned out (Illus. 55).

Illus. 55

Gather the remaining cards one on top of the other in their natural order:

$$
\begin{array}{ccc}
1 & 2 & 3 \\
4 & 5 & 6
\end{array}
$$

Or you may gather them up in reverse order—either way will work.

Have Myrna give the packet as many complete cuts as she wants. "Now, without looking at it, please place the top card face down right next to the king and queen of hearts."

After she's done this, continue (with appropriate pauses): "Place the top card on the bottom, and put the next card down in front of you. Place the next card on the bottom, and place the next card on top of the one you just put down. Place the next card on the bottom, and place the next card on the pile."

When she gets down to one card, say, "Place the next card on the bottom. Whoops! That's going to be really hard to do." Pause. "You set aside one card. Let's see if we have a match."

Yes. The card she's holding is the loving mate to the one she set aside. These two are turned face up and are placed, fanned out, next to the king and queen of hearts.

"Let's try again. Without looking at it, place the top card face down by the face-up couples. Now place the top card on the bottom, and put the next card down. . . ."

Myrna's last card is shown to match the one she set aside. These two are displayed with the others, fanned out. And the two dealt to the table are turned over and added to the display.

Don't neglect the display! It makes a colorful, satisfying conclusion.

Face-Card Foolery

This is Phil Goldstein's variation of a puzzling trick.

Remove from a deck the jack, queen, and king of these suits: clubs, spades, diamonds. Separate them into three face-up groups, according to their suits. Say, "Notice that we have the jack, queen, king of clubs; the jack, queen, king of spades; and the jack, queen, king of diamonds." Turn to

Emma. "Please select one of the suits, Emma. Then pick up the three cards of that suit, turn them face down, and mix the three, sort of shuffling them." When she finishes, say, "Please deal the three cards into a face-down row."

She is then to mix another group of the same suit and deal one on top of each card in the row, in any order she wishes. Finally, she does the same with the last group of three.

Continue the directions with appropriate pauses: "Now gather the cards, placing one pile on top of another in any order you wish. Give the pile a complete cut, and then another complete cut if you wish. Deal the cards into two piles, alternating. Put either pile on top of the other." She can repeat this cutting-and-dealing procedure any number of times.

When she's ready, take the cards from Emma, saying, "I cannot possibly know the position of any card in this group. Nevertheless, I'll attempt to separate the cards into suits by using the *names* of the suits. We'll start with the club suit."

Spell the word CLUB, moving one card from top to bottom of the packet for each letter except the last. On the last letter—the B—deal the card to the table instead of placing it on the bottom of the packet.

"Now the spade suit." Spell SPADE in the same way, dealing the last card—the E—onto the table, to the right of the first card.

"Next, the diamond suit."

Spell DIAMOND, placing the last card to the right of the others on the table.

"Let's go back the other way. First, the club."

Spell CLUB, placing the last card on top of the card *on the right.* Spell SPADE, placing the last card on top of the middle card. Spell DIAMOND, placing the last card on top of the card on the left.

"Only three left . . . We may as well just deal these out."

Without spelling, the last three cards are dealt out, going

from right to left. Turn over the piles, showing that each one contains a trio of the same suit.

This trick should be repeated *at least* once.

Ron Frame came up with an interesting variation; I added the handling.

You've performed the basic trick twice, and are about to reveal that the suits have gathered together for the third time. Pick up one of the piles and turn it over, showing that the three are all of the same suit. As you do so, move a card or two so that the three are set up in king-jack-queen order. By way of cover, as you move the cards about, say, "See? Each and every card is of the same suit." Turn the pile face down.

Pick up another pile and set it up in the same way. Turn it face down and place it on top of the first pile you showed.

Do the same with the third pile.

Emma then goes through the cutting and dealing, exactly as in the basic trick. You perform the spelling procedure as in the basic trick. As you do so, say, "Cards are very unpredictable. I wonder if something different will happen this time."

Something different *does* happen: The kings, queens, and jacks are all in separate piles. Quit at this point.

Note

In the climactic trick, the order in which you arrange the three cards doesn't matter, so long as it's consistent in all three groups. I choose the king-jack-queen order because it's less obvious.

Gotcha!

Most so-called "sucker" tricks should be reserved for times when you have an obnoxious spectator. You can do only one sucker trick for a particular group, obviously, because your victim is unlikely to take the bait twice.

"Second Deal"

For this one, you must have an odious onlooker who's eager to catch you. Apparently you show the top card and then deal off the second card from the top in an extremely sloppy "second deal." The victim *knows* that the card on the table is not the card you claim it is.

The method is quite simple. You apparently show the top card. Actually, you perform a double-lift. (See *Double-Lift,* p. 29.) You name the card. Then you make sure full attention is paid to your sloppy deal by saying, "I will now deal the card onto the table."

Very obviously push off the top card with your left thumb and pull the second card out with your right thumb (Illus. 56).

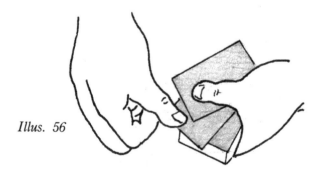

Illus. 56

Pull the top card back with your left thumb. Actually, you're performing a "legitimate" second deal, only you're making it as sloppy as possible.

Look as smug as you can. Turn to the obnoxious spectator and say, "Can you remember what this card is?"

Don't let anyone turn the card over. Put your hand over it if you have to.

The intended victim will probably say that it's not the card you claim it is. But if he doesn't, simply say, "Does everyone agree that this is the seven of hearts?" Or whatever card. If no one disagrees, say, "You're right." Show the card and continue with something else.

But it's your lucky day. The victim caught it all; he knows exactly what happened. This is definitely not the card; you dealt a second. Show the card and pause for a few seconds before the next trick so that you can enjoy the other spectators complimenting your dupe on his perspicacity.

No Wonder

Have Karen select a card, show it around, and return it to the deck. Bring it to the top. (See *Controlling a Card,* p. 13.)

Say, "Let's see if we can locate your card, Karen."

Double-lift, showing the second card from the top. (See *Double-Lift,* p. 29.) Suppose this card is the three of hearts. Say, "Let's use the three of hearts to help us." Turn over the double card on top of the deck. Take the top card (the chosen one) and hand it face down to Karen. Say, "Just stick it face down partway into the deck."

After she does so, fan through to the partially inserted card (the one selected). Set aside the cards above it, remove the inserted card, and put it face down near Karen. Turn over the next card, asking if it's the one selected. Naturally, the answer is no.

Have Karen pick up the face-down (selected) card and insert it partway into the deck face down again. Once more it fails to locate the chosen card. You might even do it a third time. Finally, hand Karen the face-down card and say, "What was your card?" When she names it, say, "Well, no wonder it didn't work." Indicate that she is to turn the card face up.

If Karen should turn over the card sometime during the procedure, ask her why she seems startled. When she points out that it is her card, say sardonically, "Wonderful! Now this will *never* work."

Spectators will be amused by either conclusion.

Dunbury Delusion

Your potential victim, Mervin, has been trying to spoil your every trick. Have him select a card and show it around. Mervin is quite capable of lying about his chosen card just to goof you up, so it's vital with this trick that all spectators know the name of the card. When the card is returned, bring it to the top. (See *Controlling a Card,* p. 13.)

Now give a lengthy speech. Near the end, you'll prepare for a sleight.

"This is the only experiment I do with cards which never fails. *Never* fails. And why? Because I've learned to tell when a spectator is lying and when he's telling the truth. Now, Mervin, I am going to cut the cards three times. The first time I'll cut a card of the same suit as your card, the second time a card of the same value, and the third time a card that will help us find your card.

"When I cut the cards, Mervin, I'll ask you a question which you are to answer yes or no. Nothing more. You may lie or tell the truth. It doesn't matter, because I'll be able to tell if you're lying or not. That's why this experiment never fails. If something has gone wrong, I'll be able to tell and can make an adjustment. Remember, just yes or no. And you can lie or tell the truth."

As you near the end of the speech, casually perform an overhand shuffle, in-jogging the first card and shuffling off. The card above the chosen card is now in-jogged. (See *Controlling a Group of Cards,* p. 22.)

You're about to perform *Drop Sleight* (p. 28). The preparation is slightly different from that described, however. Hold the deck in dealing position in your left hand. Grip the deck from above with your right hand, fingers at the front and thumb at the rear. Lift up at the jogged card with the right thumb so that you're holding a break above the chosen card with the tips of your left fingers along the right side and your right thumb at the rear (Illus. 57). The cards above the break

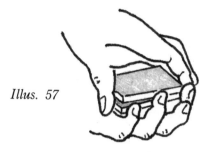

Illus. 57

should be bent up slightly at the rear with your right thumb, letting a card drop off. With the aid of the third and fourth fingers of your left hand, adjust the cards so that your right thumb grips the top section along with the card which has been dropped at the rear (Illus. 58).

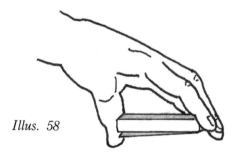

Illus. 58

For clarity, the left hand isn't shown.

You say, "Now the first card I cut will tell me the suit of your card."

Lift off the cards above the break with your right hand.

Shove over the chosen card with your left thumb. (Let's assume the card is the four of hearts.) Flip it face up with the left edge of the cards in your right hand.

"See, the four of hearts."

As you continue talking, perform the drop sleight.

"This tells me that your card is a heart. Yes or no?"

As Mervin answers, thumb the card face down onto the table. Place the lower packet on *top* of the pile in your right hand, lifting the first finger to permit passage. The chosen card, presumably on the table, is now on top.

Chances are, Mervin's answer will be yes. It doesn't matter. If he says no, smile confidently and say, "Sure."

Cut the deck at random and flip over another card (the eight of clubs). Name the card and flip it face down. Thumb it face down next to the first card, and return the packet *below* the one in your right hand, so that the chosen card remains on top.

Meanwhile, comment, "This means that your card is an eight. Yes or no?" If he says yes, say, "Of course it is." Chances are he'll say no, to which you respond, "I can tell you're lying by that almost undetectable, sneaky little smile." In either instance, reassure him that this is the one trick you do which never fails.

Again you cut off a pile of cards and flip over the card you cut to. Name it, flip it face down, thumb it off onto the table next to the other two. The pile in the left hand is returned below the one in your right so that the chosen card remains on top.

Let's assume that the third card you cut to was the seven of spades. "Ah, here we have the seven of spades. This means that your card is seventh from the top. Yes or no? No need to answer. Of course it is. Now watch this as I magically move it from the seventh position to the very top of the deck." Give the cards a false shuffle or a false cut.

Lift off the top card and hold it face down. "And now the

key question. Here we have your chosen card. Yes or no?"

Whatever the response, ask, "What is your card?" When he names it, turn the card over, announcing, "See? The one effect I achieve that never fails."

Watch them dive for that first card you dealt on the table!

Notes

Sometimes when you cut the second card, it's the same suit or value as the chosen card. This won't do. If it's the same suit, you're saying that this *is* the chosen card. If it's the same value, you're saying that you know that the first card you ostensibly placed down is the chosen one. So simply say, "Whoops, wrong card!" Continue cutting until you get one of a different suit and value.

Save the "sucker" tricks for severe cases. The best response to most irritating spectators is simply to perform your tricks well.

Recovery

An Out

The spectator names his selected card; you turn over the one in your hand, and it's the wrong one. Here's a way out.

Show the card and return it to the deck, asking, "Are you sure the five of spades was your card?" Fan through the cards so that no one else can see the faces. "It must be here somewhere."

What you want to do is bring the chosen card second from the top. Fan several cards from the bottom and transfer them to the top in a bunch. Continue doing this until you come to the chosen card. Fan one card beyond it and put that group on top. Confess, "No luck."

Turn the deck face down in the dealing position in your left hand. Take the top card and turn it face up. As you do so, push off the second card (the chosen one) slightly with your left thumb and then draw it back, taking a slight break under it with your left little finger.

Immediately place the card in your right hand face up on the deck. Square the ends of the deck with your right fingers and thumb. The two cards are now as one, separated slightly from the rest of the deck by the tip of your little finger.

"Obviously your card isn't on top." Grasp the double card with your right hand from above, thumb at the rear, second finger at the front, and first finger resting on top. Dig your left thumb beneath the deck and flip the deck face up. Place the double card underneath, presumably replacing on top the card you've just shown (Illus. 59). Carefully even up the deck, say-

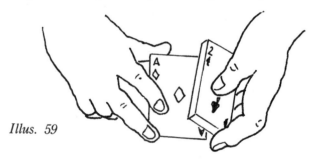

Illus. 59

ing, "And equally obviously, your card isn't on the bottom. Watch for your card."

Fan ten or so cards from the bottom. "It's not among these." Turn these cards face down and put them on the back of the deck (Illus. 60). Continue this way all through the

Illus. 60

deck. The last group you take includes all the cards up to the first face-down card. Presumably, you've shown every card in the deck, and the chosen card isn't among them. Actually, it's at your disposal on top of the deck.

How do you reveal it? You might do *Sneaky Slide* (p. 37), in which you double-lift the top card, showing that the chosen card is still not there. Then you lift off the top card, slide it through the deck edgewise, and turn it over, showing that it has changed to the chosen card.

A second possibility is one which is also a good trick on its own merits. Put the deck into your pocket. Remove a card from the bottom and place it on the table. *Rapidly* continue doing this, saying, "Tell me when to stop." Make sure you get your hand back to your pocket when the spectator says stop, so that you can pull out the top card and flip it over face up.

A third possibility is to force the chosen card on your assistant, causing him to choose the same card again. You may use the standard force or one of the surefire forces. (See *Force*, p. 23.)

MASTERY LEVELS CHART & INDEX

Lucky 7	96	*		
Magnificent Seven	57	*		
Mind Meld	84	*		
My Mistake	37		*	
No Wonder	117			*
One Ahead	82	*		
One in Four	44			*
Pop-Up Card	101		*	
Queen of India	63		*	
Quick Trick	25		*	
Quite Quaint Queens	54	*		
Royal Following	68		*	
Second Deal	116		*	
Set 'em Up	88			*
Sneaky Aces	66		*	
Sneaky Signal	81	*		
Sneaky Slide	37		*	
Something Old	61		*	
Spin-Out!	67			*
Stay Put!	41			*
Ten Tells	83	*		
That's Right, You're Wrong	38		*	
Those Mysterious Ladies	102			*
Top or Bottom Force	73		*	
Travelling Hearts	46			*
Two-Faced Card Trick—1	91	*		